A PASSION FOR GOD'S REIGN

A PASSION FOR GOD'S REIGN

*Theology, Christian Learning,
and the Christian Self*

JÜRGEN MOLTMANN
Nicholas Wolterstorff
Ellen T. Charry

Edited by
Miroslav Volf

WILLIAM B. EERDMANS PUBLISHING COMPANY
GRAND RAPIDS, MICHIGAN / CAMBRIDGE, U.K.

© 1998 Wm. B. Eerdmans Publishing Co.
255 Jefferson Ave. S.E., Grand Rapids, Michigan 49503 /
P.O. Box 163, Cambridge CB3 9PU U.K.

Printed in the United States of America

03 02 01 00 99 98   7 6 5 4 3 2 1

Library of Congress Cataloging-in-Publication Data

Moltmann, Jürgen.
A passion for God's reign: theology, Christian learning,
and the Christian self /
Jürgen Moltmann, Nicholas Wolterstorff, Ellen T. Charry.
p.   cm.
Includes bibliographical references.
ISBN 0-8028-4494-4 (pbk.: alk. paper)
1. Theology, Doctrinal.   2. Religion and civilization.
3. Civilization, Modern — 20th century.
4. Civilization, Western — 20th century.
I. Wolterstorff, Nicholas.   II. Charry, Ellen T.   III. Title.
BT78.M76 1998
230'.09'03 — dc21   97-38349
                                              CIP

Contents

Introduction

MIROSLAV VOLF

In the fascinating novel, *The Curious Enlightenment of Professor Caritat,* Steven Lukes, a professor of political and social theory, tells the story of Nicholas Caritat, a scholar of the Enlightenment and therefore, Caritat reasons, a man with no role in the political struggle in Militaria, the autocratic state in which he lives. He is wrong. In the space of twenty-four hours, Caritat is arrested by the police, then liberated by the guerrillas of the Visible Hand. They give him the code name Pangloss and send him on a mission that only a philosopher could undertake: to find the best of all possible worlds. Lukes's book is about Professor Caritat's journey from the country of Militaria through the countries of Utilitaria, Communitaria, Libertaria, a dream visit to Proletaria, and about readjustments he makes to his original Enlightenment vision in the course of his journeys.[1]

One way to think about the essays in this book is to say that they are seeking to explore what Caritat could have learned — what

---

1. Steven Lukes, *The Curious Enlightenment of Professor Caritat: A Comedy of Ideas* (London and New York: Verso, 1995).

he *ought* to have learned — had he undertaken a journey into the country we may call "Christiania." In Lukes's book, Christiania does not get a chapter, as do Communitaria and Libertaria, for instance; it is not even mentioned. In a sense, this is exactly right. Properly understood, Christian faith is not strictly speaking an alternative to Communitarianism or Liberalism, or any other political philosophy for that matter. It would be a category mistake to understand Christian faith as a political philosophy (just as it is a category mistake to understand the church as *polis* or as "culture"). Rather, Christian faith has bearing on and demands creative development of political philosophies that will vary depending on the cultural, social, and economic contexts for which they are developed. But if we take "Christiania" to mean not a full-blown political philosophy but a set of commitments derived from faith in the crucified and resurrected Messiah of God, then we may well see this book as an exploration of what the journey to Christiania would do to the original Enlightenment social vision and what has come of it in the course of the centuries.

Without wanting to rob the reader of the thrill of discovery, I want to state in advance what Caritat would *not* find if he took a journey into the Christiania of the present book. First, none of the authors shares the original Enlightenment vision "of the human race, at last released from the empire of fate and from the enemies of its progress, advancing with a firm and sure step along the path of virtue, truth and happiness" (pp. 29-30). So if Caritat remained committed to the Enlightenment after the journey into Christiania, he would be committed to some "curious Enlightenment," as the title of Lukes's novel puts it. Second, none of the authors shares the pseudo-Christian obverse of this Enlightenment vision, in Lukes's novel represented by a priest who visits Caritat in Militaria's prison. Caritat is not so happy about the visit; he prefers "clarity to consolation" and objects to the "blind faith" of the priest. Nevertheless, the priest sits at the end of his bed and, among other things, explains why he does not share the Enlightenment's "articles of faith," written, as he puts it, "by people lost in illusions." "The domain of human action," he says, "is entirely governed by two great principles: Perversity and Futility. The first guarantees that good intentions pave the road to Hell, that attempts to make this world better are certain only to make it worse. The second ensures that all roads marked 'Progress' or 'Reform' lead nowhere and run into the sand. Any map that indicates otherwise is not a map of this world" (pp. 29ff.). When Professor Caritat objects that the priest has a "Pessimistic vision," the priest responds with laughter: "'So you think I am a Pessimist. Let me tell you,' he leant forward with an intent expression, 'a Pessimist says: "Things could not be worse." An Optimist says: "Oh yes, they could." In this sense, I am a resolute Optimist'" (p. 34).

As the editor of this volume I want to invite you on a journey somewhere between these two options, between the original vision of the Enlightenment and the strange, utterly pessimistic optimism of the priest. But before I leave you with Moltmann, Wolterstorff, and Charry to explore how Christian faith relates to some significant aspects of modernity, I need to make you aware of some institutions and people without whom this journey would not have been possible. In the framework of its regular Payton lectures, Fuller Theological Seminary hosted the conference on "Christianity and Western Values" (April 19-20, 1996) at which all chapters of this book, except the first, were presented as papers. William B. Eerdmans Publishing Company subsidized the conference with a generous grant and has worked with much dedication and expertise on the production of the book; Mr. Jon Pott deserves special mention. Finally, Ms. Medi Sorterup tracked down a number of English translations of Moltmann's original quotations, and Ms. Jill Colwell helped with editing Moltmann's texts.

And now the journey.

Theology in the Project of the Modern World

JÜRGEN MOLTMANN

1. What Is Theology, and What Is Its Function?

It is simple, but true, to say that theology has only one, single problem: God. We are theologians for the sake of God; if we are not, then we ought not to call ourselves theologians at all. God is our dignity. God is our agony. God is our hope.

But where is God? God is the subject of his own existence. So God is not in our religion, our culture, or our church. God is in God's own presence, in God's Spirit and in God's kingdom. Our churches, cultures, and religions are then in their own truth, if they are in God's presence. Theology for the sake of God is always kingdom-of-God theology.[1]

As kingdom-of-God theology, theology has to be public theology: the public, critical, and prophetic cry for God — the public,

---

1. In the revised edition of *A Theology of Liberation: History, Politics, and Salvation* (Maryknoll, N.Y.: Orbis, 1988), p. 227 n. 103, Gustavo Gutiérrez emphasizes that every sound theology of liberation must be rooted in the theology of the kingdom of God.

critical, and prophetic hope for God. Its public character is constitutive for theology, for the sake of the kingdom of God. Public
theology needs institutional liberty in relation to the church, and a
place in the open house of scholarship and the sciences.

Let me speak personally for a moment: theology is for me a
suffering from God and a passion for God's kingdom. For me this
is a messianic passion, because it is possessed and moved by the
presence of the crucified Christ. For me theology springs from a
divine passion — it is the open wound of God in one's own life and
in the tormented men, women, and children of this world; from
the accusation Job threw at God; from Christ's cry of forsakenness
on the cross. We are not theologians because we are particularly
religious; we are theologians because in the face of this world we
miss God. We are crying out for his righteousness and justice, and
are not prepared to come to terms with mass death on earth.

But for me theology also springs from God's love for life — the
love for life that we experience in the presence of the life-giving
Spirit and that enables us to move beyond our resignation and begin
to love life here and now. These are also Christ's two experiences of
God, the kingdom of God and the cross, and because of that they
are the foundations of Christian theology, as well: God's delight and
God's pain. It is out of the tension between these two that hope is
born for the kingdom in which God is wholly in the world and the
world is wholly in God. "Seek first the kingdom of God. . . ."

If we want to perceive the unmistakably theological, and hence
universal, task of the kingdom of God in the modern world today
and tomorrow, we have to discover the implicit theology of this
"modern world" of ours. We have to understand why and how it
was born, so that we can recognize its vitality as well as its congenital
defects. The modern world is a child of Jewish and Christian hope.
So in the second part of my essay I want to talk about the birth of
the modern world from the spirit of messianic hope.

It is not the pluralism of modern times that is the only problem for the postmodern world. The other problem is the polarization between modernity and submodernity. So in the third part I should like to talk about the contradiction between modernity and submodernity or the end times of the modern world.

Finally I shall try to define afresh the tasks of kingdom-of-God theology. Let's reinvent modernity! So in the fourth part I shall talk about the rebirth of the world from the Spirit of life.

2. The Birth of the Modern World from the Spirit of Messianic Hope

The "new time" *(Neuzeit)* of the modern world has at least two significant origins: (1) the *conquista,* the discovery and conquest of America from 1492 onwards; (2) the scientific and technological seizure of power over nature by human beings.

1. In 1492 the foundation was laid for the new world order that still exists today. At that time Europe moved from a fairly peripheral existence into the center of the world. The year 1492 was the beginning of the European seizure of power over other peoples and continents, and, according to Hegel, the hour when modern times were born.[2] The Spaniards and Portuguese, then the English, the Dutch, the French in the Americas, Africa, and Asia, and the Russians in Siberia, all "discovered" a new world for themselves, some in the West, the others in the East.

What does "discover" mean? To "discover" something means more than simply finding something that has been hidden. It always

2. G. W. F. Hegel, *The Philosophy of History* (New York: Colonial, 1900), p. 86: "America is therefore the land of the future, where, in the ages that lie before us, the burden of the World's History shall reveal itself." Paul Kennedy, in *The Rise and Fall of the Great Powers* (New York: Vintage, 1987), describes well how insignificant European peoples were in comparison with the Ottoman kingdom, the Indian moguls' realm, or China in 1492.

means an appropriation of what has been discovered and is therefore marked with the name of the discoverer. America was not just located, as it were; it was appropriated, and molded according to the will of its "discoverers."[3] "America [is] an invention of European thinking," says the Mexican historian Edmundo O'Gorman. The conquistadores found what they were looking for, because they invented it. The real life and real civilizations of the Aztecs, Mayas, and Incas were never discovered at all; rather, as "other" and "alien" they were repressed and sacrificed.[4] Islands, mountains, and rivers had long since been given indigenous names. But Columbus "baptized" them with Spanish, Christian names, and to give something a name is to take possession of it. The same can be said about the suppression of the languages of the "discovered peoples." Not least, the myth of "unclaimed property," "no-man's land," and "the wilderness" legalized the robbery and the colonizations.

With the conquest of America, European Christianity also arrived at worldwide domination. It won souls not for the gospel but for the Christian empire. The decisive question was not belief or unbelief; it was baptism or death.[5]

2. The seizure of power over nature by means of science and technology is the second foundation stone of the new world order. In the century between Copernicus and Sir Isaac Newton, the new sciences robbed nature of her divine mystery, which until then had

3. See B. Dietschy, "Die Tücken des Entdeckens: Ernst Bloch, Kolumbus und die Neue Welt," *Jahrbuch der Ernst-Bloch-Gesellschaft* (1992/93): 234-51.

4. A. W. Crosby, *Ecological Imperialism: The Biological Expansion of Europe, 900-1900* (Cambridge: Cambridge University Press, 1986); Enrique Dussel, *The Invention of the Americas: Eclipse of "the Other" and the Myth of Modernity* (New York: Continuum, 1995).

5. Tzvetan Todorov, *The Conquest of America: The Question of the Other* (New York: HarperCollins, 1984); Douglas E. Stannard, *American Holocaust: Columbus and the Quest of the New World* (New York: Oxford University Press, 1992).

been called *anima mundi,* the "world soul."[6] All the taboos arising from the awe of "Mother Earth" and the greatness of life were then swept away. Here, too, "discoveries" are made, marked with the name of the discoverers, and are rewarded down to the present day with Nobel prizes. This scientific process of "discovery" does not just put an end to our ignorance. It sets objects in relation to us ourselves. Modern scientific reason is instrumentalizing reason, reason whose epistemological drive is utilization and domination.[7] This pushed out the older receptive reason, which was an organ of perception, and the earlier *phronēsis,* which clothed reason in wisdom. According to Kant's *Critique of Pure Reason,* modern reason now sees only "what it itself has brought forth according to its own design," by "compelling nature to give an answer to its questions" (preface to the second edition). This "compulsion" of nature is called "experiment," and in the eighteenth century it was often compared with inquisition under torture. Right down to the present day Bacon's motto holds true: "Knowledge is power." And today genetic knowledge has become the power over life.

From science and technology Europe acquired that instrumentalizing knowledge which enabled it to use the resources of the colonized world to build up a worldwide civilization. Today the origins of this civilization are no longer evident, because it looks just the same in Frankfurt, Chicago, and Singapore. The victorious march of science and technology lent Christianity the status of being the religion of the victorious God. In the nineteenth century, a

6. For the idea of a "world soul," see Heinz Robert Schlette, *Weltseele, Geschichte und Hermeneutik* (Frankfurt: J. Knecht, 1993); Carolyn Merchant, *The Death of Nature: Women, Ecology and the Scientific Revolution* (New York: Harper-Collins, 1989).

7. Max Horkheimer and Theodor W. Adorno, *Dialectic of Enlightenment* (New York: Continuum, 1974); Max Horkheimer, *Critical Theory: Selected Essays* (New York: Continuum, 1995); Jürgen Habermas, *Knowledge and Human Interests* (Boston: Beacon, 1971).

victorious, expanding Western civilization called its age "the Christian Century."

What hope motivated the modern European discoveries of the world? It was the vision of the New World.

Columbus was evidently seeking both God's Garden of Eden and Eldorado, the city of gold.[8] God and gold were the most powerful incentives of the *conquista*.[9] The city of gold that Columbus and the rest were looking for was not simply intended for their personal enrichment. Columbus also defended his search for gold as a way of winning back Jerusalem, appealing to Joachim of Fiore's prophecy: "From Spain will come those who will bring back the ark to Zion." Jerusalem was going to be the capital of the thousand-years' empire of Christ. Columbus also believed more firmly than other people in the earthly paradise. When he saw the rolling hills that surround what is now Venezuela, he shrank back, writing in 1498: "There is the earthly paradise which no one can attain unless it is God's will." He understood his mission in both messianic and apocalyptic terms, like the many conquerors and settlers in America after him: it was the "new heaven and the new earth," or — as people in America were accustomed to say — "the new world," *Novus ordo seclorum,* as it is written on the seal of the United States. America always excited the utopian fantasy of Europe profoundly. The best-known examples are Sir Thomas More's *Utopia* (1516), which drew on the travel accounts of Amerigo Vespucci, and Tommaso Campanella's *Civitas solis* (1623), which took the Incan sun state as its model. And the "American Dream" was first dreamt in the slums and during the depressions of Europe.

---

8. Ernst Bloch, *The Principle of Hope* (Cambridge: MIT Press, 1986), pp. 746-47. Dietschy ("Tücken," pp. 238ff.) characterized these ideas as "the inner-worldly eschatology of modernity."

9. Gustavo Gutierrez, *Las Casas: In Search of the Poor of Jesus Christ* (Maryknoll, N.Y.: Orbis, 1993).

What hope motivated modern civilization? It is the vision of the New Time.

The interpretative framework that mobilized Europe's various seizures of power over the world and gave them their orientation was millenarian expectation: the expectation that when Christ comes, the saints will reign with him for a thousand years and will judge the nations, and that this empire of Christ's will be the last, golden age of humanity in history before the end of the world.[10] In the United States there is no need to stress the degree to which the Pilgrim fathers and the pious immigrants who settled North America and wiped out the Indians were molded by millenarian expectations.[11] Even today, American presidents invoke in their inaugural addresses "the messianic faith of our fathers"; and "the millennial role of America" is still easily detectable in the political philosophy of the United States.

Through immigration Europeans, recently joined by Asian peoples, founded the United States, formed its culture, and made this country the central country. Afro-Americans came as slaves but brought their liberation into American life. The United States is a unique experiment of humankind: *E pluribus unum,* and therefore also a unique danger for the "rest of the world."[12]

At the beginning of modern times a wave of messianic hope swept through the whole of Europe. We find it in the Jewish messianism of Shabbatai Tzebi, in the Puritan apocalypse, in seven-

---

10. Jürgen Moltmann, *The Coming of God: Christian Eschatology* (Minneapolis: Fortress Press, 1996), pp. 129-255.

11. Ernest Lee Tuveson, *Redeemer Nation: The Idea of America's Millennial Role* (Chicago: University of Chicago Press, 1968); M. Darrel Bryant and Donald W. Dayton, eds., *The Coming Kingdom: Essays in American Millennialism and Eschatology* (New York: Rose of Sharon, 1983).

12. This means the obverse of American millenarianism: the modern apocalyptic of the doomsday literature. See as an example the bestseller by Hal Lindsey, *The Late Great Planet Earth* (Grand Rapids: Zondervan, 1970).

teenth-century "prophetic theology," and in German Pietism
(Comenius, Spener, Bengel, Oetinger).[13] There have always been
millennial end-time expectations in Christianity. But with the beginning of the modern era, the new time signal was heard. The time
of fulfillment is now; this hope can be realized today. Thus following
Joachim of Fiore's vision, modern times were called in Germany
Neuzeit —("new time." "Ancient times" and "medieval times" had
now been succeeded by the "new time," which is the end time and
"the third age" of the Spirit who is God within us.[14]

World history is being "consummated" now. Humanity is being
perfected now. Progress in every sector is beginning now. The lordship of the saints over the nations is going to be realized now; the
lordship of human beings over the earth will be restored now.
Science and technology are now giving back to human beings what
they lost through original sin: *dominium terrae,* as Francis Bacon
put it — domination over the earth. Human beings are coming of
age now. The human being is good, and by education can become
morally better and better. This Enlightenment optimism about the
human race is based on a millenarian conviction: "In this final age
Satan has been bound for a thousand years," so that the good can
spread unhindered.

Lessing's "Thoughts on the Education of the Human Race"
("Gedanken über die Erziehung des Menschengeschlechts," 1780)

---

13. See Jacob Taubes, *Abendländische Eschatologie* (1947; Munich: Matthes
und Seitz, 1991); Richard Bauckham, *Tudor Apocalypse: Sixteenth Century Apoc-
alypticism, Millenarianism and the English Reformation: From John Bale to John
Foxe and Thomas Brightman* (Oxford: Sutton Courtenay Press, 1975). *Spes Israelis*
(1650), the book of the chief rabbi of Amsterdam, Manasseh ben Israel, which
was dedicated to Oliver Cromwell and resulted in permission for the Jews to
return to England, was highly influential. Marjorie Reeves, in *Joachim of Fiore
and the Prophetic Future* (London: SPCK, 1976), shows how strongly the spirit
of Joachim influenced English Protestantism and the English Enlightenment.

14. Lutz Niethammer, *Posthistoire: Has History Come to an End?* (New York:
Verso, 1992); Francis Fukuyama, *The End of History* (New York: Free Press, 1991).

became the foundational document of the German Enlightenment. It is messianic through and through.[15] Lessing proclaimed nothing less than "the third age" of the Spirit, which Joachim had promised, and with it the consummation of history. This era begins when all reasonable people pass from a merely "historical faith in the church" to "a general faith in reason" — a faith in which all human beings recognize the truth, simply of their own accord, without the mediation of the church, and when everyone does what is good without the church's guidance, simply because it is good. Religion's "divine plan of salvation" had turned into the progress of history. For Kant, the French Revolution, with its solemn praise of humanity — "all human beings created free and equal" — and its democracy, was the "historical sign" of the development of a better humanity. "We see," he declared, "that the philosophers can have their chiliasm too."[16] For Kant, this meant the "perfect civil union of the human race" into a "covenant of nations" *(foedus amphictyonum)* that would guarantee "eternal peace," an idea that in the Declarations on Human Rights and in the policy of the United Nations has come to be seen as an inescapable necessity if humanity is to survive.

If we look at the messianism of modern times, we can understand why for Kant the religious question was not: What links us with our origin? or: What gives me a hold on eternity? The real question was: What can I hope for?[17] It is only a future that we are allowed to hope for that gives any meaning to life in history and to all historical experiences and actions. For modernity, the hoped-for future is a new paradigm of transcendence.

15. Fritz Gerlich, *Der Kommunismus als Lehre vom Tausendjährigen Reich* (Munich: H. Bruckmann, 1921), has shown that Lessing was influenced by the pietistic chiliasm of the philosopher Chr. A. Crusius.

16. Immanuel Kant, *On History* (Indianapolis: Bobbs-Merrill, 1963).

17. Immanuel Kant, *Critique of Pure Reason*, A 805: "All the interests of my reason, speculative as well as practical, combine in the three following questions: 1. What can I know? 2. What ought I to do? 3. What may I hope?"

3. Contradictions between Modernity and Submodernity

In our credulous faith in progress it is easy to rush precipitously from modernity into "postmodernity," but it is more realistic to pause first, and to be clear about the victims of modernity in "submodernity." History's fine messianic upper side has its ugly apocalyptic underside; the victorious advance of the European nations has meant the retreat of the other nations, with all the loss involved, and the development of the culture of pure reason has led to the subjugation of the bodies, the feelings, and the senses of modern people. The success story of the "First World" has been accompanied by the story of suffering of the Third. We need only compare dates and simultaneous events. When in 1517 Luther nailed up his Theses on the door of the church in Wittenberg and the Reformation in Germany began, Hernan Cortés was sailing to Tenochtitlán (Mexico). In 1521, when he conquered the city of the Aztecs, Luther was banned and excommunicated by the Reichstag in Worms *(Reichsacht und Kirchenbann)*. When Lessing and Kant were publishing their Enlightenment treatises, more than two million black African slaves were being sold every year to the Americas. And we might go on.

The industrial development of the modern world was always at the cost of the earth's destruction, as the ravaged industrial landscapes in the Ruhr, in north and central England, in Pennsylvania, and in Siberia show. So the progress of the modern world has always been solely at the expense of other nations *and* at the expense of nature — *and* today at the expense of coming generations, too. If the real costs had had to be met, the actual progress made would have been very small.

Only one-third of the modern world is the modern "First World." Two-thirds of it are the modern "Third World." Modern times — German's "new time" — have produced both modernity and submodernity. For the oppressed people in the countries of the

Third World, and for the exploited and silenced earth, the messianism of modern times was never anything but the apocalypse of their annihilation. The memories of the perpetrators are always and everywhere short, while the memories of the victims are long. But because our divided human worlds are inextricably linked, and because no human civilization can cut itself free from the ecosystems of the earth we all share, the downfall of the Third World means the downfall of the First World too, and the destruction of the earth will also mean the extinction of the human race.

1. *The economic end time.* I said that the Third World came into existence when the modern world began. In fact, it was only the modern mass enslavement of Africans and the exploitation of Latin America's mineral resources that provided the labor and capital for the development and advancement of the Western or First World.[18] From the seventeenth century until well into the nineteenth, Europe's wealth was built up on the basis of a great transcontinental, triangular commerce: slaves from Africa to America; gold and silver from America to Europe, followed by sugar, cotton, coffee, and rubber; then industrial commodities and weapons to Africa, and so on. This transatlantic commerce produced the investment capital for the industrialization of western Europe. Through the slave trade it destroyed the cultures and wealth of western Africa, and through monocultures it destroyed the native subsistence economies of Central and South America, rendering whole peoples into the victims of European development.

The consequences are familiar enough. Only yesterday the direct exploitation of labor and natural resources had already been replaced by the burden of an enormous debt that has to be repaid. Yet today

18. See Eduardo Galeano, *Open Veins of Latin America: Five Centuries of the Pillage of a Continent* (New York: Monthly Review Press, 1973). For a history of slavery, see Daniel Pratt Mannix, *Black Cargoes: A History of the Atlantic Slave Trade* (New York: Viking, 1962).

the automation of production is making industry increasingly independent of the low wages and cheap labor in the poorer countries. More and more countries in Africa and Latin America are ceasing to be of any concern at all to the industrial North. The exploited Third World is being turned into a superfluous backwoods and the people into "surplus people." We see the first sign of this road to extermination in "the coming anarchy" in Africa, which Robert D. Kaplan described so movingly in his article in the *Atlantic Monthly* of February 1994.[19] Western African states dissolve and become ungovernable. Ecological destruction is driving the masses into the slums of the megacities, and epidemic plagues return. An enormous poverty movement is going to develop that will push forward into the richer countries, and these will become fortresses that protect themselves against the intrusive masses by way of "new iron curtains": the fortress of Europe, the fortress of Japan, the fortress of North America, and so on. What I do see coming are crusades of the poor against the rich countries, and the decimation of surplus people through famine and disease. In this struggle for existence on an overpopulated earth, culture and religion will be no more than a means to an end.

2. *The ecological end time.* As Bill McKibben said, the beginning of the modern world is also the beginning of "the end of nature."[20] The modern world emerged from the scientific discovery and technical mastery of nature, and today it is living from that more than ever.

The spread of scientific and technological civilization as we have hitherto known it is leading to the annihilation of more and more plant and animal species. In the last sixty years the human popula-

19. R. D. Kaplan, "The Coming Anarchy," *Atlantic Monthly* 273 (February 1994): 44-76.

20. William Leiss, *The Domination of Nature* (New York: Braziller, 1972); Bill McKibben, *The End of Nature* (New York: Random House, 1989).

tion of the world has quadrupled, and at the beginning of the next century it will number eight to ten billion people. The foodstuffs required and the waste produced will rise accordingly. Urbanization will rise from 29 percent in 1950 to 46.6 percent in the year 2000. Deforestation continues, and the deserts are growing. The human ecosystem has lost its equilibrium and is well on the way to destroying the earth and itself. Unless we make radical changes, it is easy to extrapolate from the facts and trends of the present crises to the ecological collapse of the earth.[21]

The modern civilization that began in Europe is an expansionist culture toward other countries and toward nature. Earlier "premodern" or non-European societies, which are now called "underdeveloped," cherished the wisdom of self-restriction and the preservation of equilibriums between civilization and nature, but this wisdom has been lost.

This brings us to the decisive questions of the present day: Is industrial society inescapably "the end of nature," or can nature be protected against industrial society? Is the biosphere the indispensable foundation of the human technosphere, or can the technosphere be so expanded that the biosphere as we have hitherto known it becomes dispensable? Should we protect nature from us human beings for its own sake, or must we reshape the earth into an artificial world, like a spacecraft, in which human beings who have been suitably adapted through genetic manipulations can go on existing? Can we change the industrial society into an ecological society?

3. *The God crisis.* It is understandable that the contradictions of the modern world should have led to profound crises of trust among modern men and women.[22] Trust in time is lost if you do not know

---

21. See the utterly pessimistic book by Gregory Fuller, *Das Ende: Von der heiteren Hoffnungalokeit im Angesicht der ökologischen Katastrophe* (Zurich: Ammann, 1993).

22. Johanness Baptist Metz, "Die Gotteskrise," in idem, *Diagnosen zur Zeit* (Düsseldorf: Patmos, 1994).

whether there will be a future. Trust in the earth is gone if the earth is contaminated. Trust in humanity is destroyed by modern mass slaughter. These frustrations are not simply religious uncertainties. Religious certainties are on offer in teeming abundance. What is at stake is a loss of the assurance of God and the self in a profounder sense. Nietzsche expressed it in 1886 with prophetic solemnity: "The greatest new event [is] that 'God is dead.'" The generations of our forefathers and foremothers experienced precisely this in the mass slaughter of the First World War, in which the most advanced European and Christian nations mowed one another down. My generation experienced it in the unimaginable horrors and the unbearable guilt of Auschwitz, where millions of Jews and other people were murdered in gas chambers with the methods of an industrial process. Today we are asking ourselves whether our progress is worth the sacrifice of the people of the Third World.

The founders of the modern age thought of a new, glorious era for the whole human race, but we are surviving in fortresses of wealth planted in a sea of mass misery. Those earlier men and women believed that all human beings "are created free and equal," but we know that our modern lifestyle cannot be universalized. The growing anarchy in the Third World matches the growing apathy of the First. Our social frigidity toward the disadvantaged and the humiliated is an expression of our frigidity toward God. The cynicism of modern manipulators is an expression of our contempt for God. We have lost God, so we are not bothered by the suffering of others that we have caused, or by the debts that we are leaving behind us for coming generations. We see all this, but it leaves us unmoved. We know it, but it does not touch us. Knowledge no longer reveals our power, but more our powerlessness. We are as if paralyzed. This growing apathy is not confined to Protestants or Catholics, Christians or Muslims, Europeans or non-Europeans. It is becoming more and more universal, and has to be based on an objective alienation from God: God has concealed his face and is far away from us.

The great dreams of humanity that accompanied the "discoveries" and the projects of modern times from their inception were necessary dreams but impossible ones. They asked too much of human beings. Mexico was not Eldorado, and the Garden of Eden was not to be found in Venezuela. The United States is not "the new world" in the messianic sense, and the modern age is not a "new time" *(Neuzeit)* in any messianic sense at all.

The scientific discovery and technical mastery of nature did not make human beings the image of God. The humanitarian notions of the Enlightenment neither improved the human race morally, nor did they "consummate" history. The images of "a brave new world" after the close of history only deepened history's wretchedness and brought the human race closer to its end. The messianism of the First World produced the apocalyptic end time of the Third World, and the end time of nature, too. We no longer know where the project of the modern world is taking us. That is the "orientation crisis" that is so often invoked. And we no longer know whether our thinking and working within this modern project ministers to life or to death. That is the "crisis of meaning" that we hear so much about.

4. The Rebirth of Modernity out of the Spirit of Life

The visions of modern times are impossible visions, but they are necessary ones. For all of us, there is only one alternative to the humanitarian ideas of human dignity and human rights, and that alternative is barbarism. There is only one alternative to the ideal of eternal peace, and that is a permanent state of war. There is only one alternative to faith in the one God and hope for his righteousness, and that is polytheism and chaos. What must we preserve from the project of modernity, and what must we reject? What must we reinvent, so that the project does not founder?

1. *Hope for God without millenarianism.* The God of the Bible, according to the book of the promises and according to the book of the gospel, is the God "who is and who was and who is to come" (Rev. 1:4). That is to say, he will appear in his full divinity only in his coming kingdom. The question is: Where has God already come? Where are we so certain of his presence that we can live and act with the assurance of God and ourselves? The messianism of modern times said: "With God we will enter into lordship over the earth, and with Christ we will judge the nations." This messianic dream became a nightmare for the people and an overcharge for the dreamers, ending in cold desperation.[23] But it is not in our domination that the coming God is present through his life-giving Spirit; it is in our hope. It is not in our power that the grace that raises us up is made perfect; it is in our weakness.

What, according to the Revelation to John, precedes the thousand-years' kingdom of Christ? Resistance against "the beast from the abyss" and the great refusal to sacrifice to the idols and laws of Babylon, or to make common cause with Babylon in enriching ourselves at the cost of other peoples. The millennium is preceded by martyrdom.[24] Only those who suffer with Christ will reign with him (2 Tim. 2:2). What the messianism of modern times has left out is the presence of the divine future in suffering, in resistance, in persecution, and in martyrdom. This fact prompted the appalling picture that made "Babylon" Christian, declaring that it itself was the thousand-years' empire. For what else does Francis Fukuyama mean when he glamorizes "the global marketing of all things and liberal democracy" as "the end of history"? We must turn back

23. Horst Eberhard Richter, *All Mighty: A Study of the God Complex in Western Man* (Claremont: Hunter House, 1984).

24. We owe to Erik Peterson the proof that Revelation has nothing to do with the end-time speculation of a theology of salvation history, but is the "Book of the Martyrs." See Erik Peterson, "Zeuge der Wahrheit," in *Theologische Traktate* (Munich: Kösel, 1951), pp. 165-24.

theologically from apocalyptical Armageddon to Christian Golgotha. It was on the historical Golgotha that Christ was victorious, not in the apocalyptic Armageddon. It is in the crucified one that the coming God is present in history. It is in christology that the final eschatological questions are decided with the certainty of faith.

Where is God? Where can we find him in this history of ours? Before his eternal kingdom dawns, the coming God is present in his *Shekinah.* When the first temple was destroyed in 585 B.C. and Israel was driven into Babylonian captivity, what was left of God's special "indwelling" in the temple? One answer was: The Shekinah of the Lord went into captivity with the people and suffered Israel's sufferings with her. God is the comrade on the way and the divine companion of his people in suffering.[25]

The gospel says that the divine Word and its eternal Wisdom became flesh in Jesus and lived among us (John 1:14). That is the Shekinah theology of the New Testament. If God lives among us, God journeys with us, too. If God journeys with us, God suffers with us as well. In suffering with us God gives us the certainty of God's self and ourselves in the great exile of this world.[26]

We are always inclined to perceive God, the Absolute, only in whatever is like ourselves. What is like us confirms us in our identity, what is alien to us makes us uncertain. That is why we love what is like ourselves, and are afraid of what is strange. That is the form which social self-righteousness takes. It is typically millenarian: God is like us — we are like God. We rule with God and God is on our victorious side.

We go a step beyond this when we try to revere and perceive God as the *Wholly Other* (Karl Barth) in what is "other" and strange

25. Peter Kuhn, *Gottes Selbsterniedrigung in der Theologie der Rabbinen* (Munich: Kösel, 1968); Arnold M. Goldberg, *Untersuchungen über die Vorstellung van der Schekhinah in der frühen rabbinischen Literatur* (Berlin: de Gruyter, 1969).

26. Jürgen Moltmann, *The Way of Jesus Christ: Christology in Messianic Dimensions* (San Francisco: Harper & Row, 1990).

(Emmanuel Levinas). We revere and perceive other people and those who are strange to us when we stop trying to make them like ourselves, but open ourselves to their particular character, and transform ourselves, together with them, into a new community of people who are different from one another. Then the acceptance of others becomes the form that social justice takes. Of course this presupposes that in our relation to God we know that we are accepted by God as those who are alienated from God, but who as alien are justified in God.

We take a step further still when we try to respect and perceive God in the victims of our own violence, perceiving him as the victim of human greed for world domination. God, the victim in the victims, is "the crucified God," who looks at us with the silent eyes of abandoned street children. When Archbishop Oscar Arnulfo Romero discovered this, he resisted — and was murdered.[27]

"God is dead — we have killed him," Nietzsche maintained. Unfortunately he did not see *when* we kill God. We kill God when we make God's image the victim of our violence, for God is in God's image. We kill God when we shut out and drive away strangers, for God is in the stranger. We kill God when we choose death instead of life and secure our own lives at the price of the death of many other living things, for God is the living God. Anyone who infringes life infringes God. Anyone who does not love life does not love God. God is a God of the whole of life, of every life and of the shared life of us all.[28]

2. *Freedom and equality for all human beings.* Humanity's modernity project began with the acknowledgment that "all human beings are created free and equal" and that "liberty, equality, and

27. Oscar A. Romero, *Die notwendige Revolution: Mit einem Beitrag van Ion Sobrino über die Märtyrer der Befreiung* (Munich and Mainz, 1982).

28. Gustavo Gutierrez, *The God of Life* (Maryknoll, N.Y.: Orbis, 1991); Jürgen Moltmann, *The Spirit of Life: A Universal Affirmation* (Minneapolis: Fortress Press, 1992).

fraternity" (and sisterhood) belong together. In the liberal democracies of the Western world we have grasped what individual liberty means over against the power of the state. But are "all human beings" free? That promise of human rights and constitutional government has certainly not as yet been realized. Many citizens' rights movements and many struggles for freedom will be needed before that promise is fulfilled. Totally unrealized, however, is the truth that "all human beings have been created equal." Because socialism made this demand of modern times its own, and so bitterly betrayed it in its party dictatorships, no one wants to talk about the "equality" of all human beings anymore — at least not their economic equality. Yet there is no universal liberty for every individual without fundamental equality for everyone. Without equality, liberty cannot be universalized. Without a degree of economic equality, there is no democracy.

What kind of equality? Equality as a social concept means justice. Without just social and political conditions there can be no peace among human beings and nations. Equality as an ethical concept means solidarity, brotherly and sisterly love — *philadelphia*, as humanism called it in so Christian a way! Is that pure idealism? I do not think so. I believe it is naked realism if humanity is to survive. Without the creation of comparable living conditions in all the countries of the world, we shall not be able to call a halt to the many refugee movements in the twenty-first century. One small, simple example is united Germany: if hundreds of thousands of Germans are not to emigrate from the east to the west, we have to create equal living conditions in east and west. That is costly, but possible. The same is true for a united Europe: in order to stop the trek from east to west, the east must be made a place where people can live. Things will be no different in the North-South conflict: we shall not be able to withstand the pressure of millions of refugees simply by way of new iron curtains. We shall be able to do so only by creating equal living conditions here and there. The social task of the future is *equality*. It is not equality "in our own image," but it is the equality that springs from recognition of other people and the reparation due to our victims.

3. *The ecological age*. Finally, we are standing before an ecological reformation of modern society and of the religion of modern human beings. It has been said that the nineteenth and twentieth centuries were the "economic age," since economic concerns were everywhere central. By contrast, the twenty-first century will become the ecological age, since the earth organism itself will become the one factor that must everywhere command respect. Management of the "world economy" will become management of the "economy of the earth" (Ernst von Weissäcker), and "global politics" will become "politics of the earth." If humankind is to survive, the human economy will have to be carried on with an eye toward the preservation of life in concordance with the ecology of the earth itself, and through restoration of whatever damage we have already inflicted on the earth, water, and air.

This ecological reformation of society will require a new spirituality and a new theological architecture. The previous mentality of dominion and exploitation will have to be replaced by a new, cosmic spirituality. Ernesto Cardenal's powerful *Cantico Cosmico* is a magnificent opening of a new spiritual world.[29] We will rediscover God's hidden immanence in nature and will respect the divine presence in all creatures. "No creature is so distant from God that it would not have God within itself" (Thomas Aquinas). "The Spirit of God fills the world" (Wis. 1:7), it keeps all life alive and together in a vivifying, supportive community.

We will leave Western anthropocentrism behind us, which declared human beings to be the "center of the world" (Pico della Mirandola). It is not the human being that is the measure of all

29. Ernesto Cardenal, *Cosmic Canticle* (Willimantic, Conn.: Curbstone Press, 1993).

things, but rather God, who created all life in order to invite all living things to the creation celebration of the sabbath. If we are able to overcome modern anthropocentrism, we will also release anew the repressed dimensions of human corporeality and its senses. The human being is more than merely a "subject of understanding and will." If we are able to reintegrate understanding and will into the body and sense perceptions, we will also be able to reintegrate human culture into the nature of the organism that is the earth. Not least, however, we must reintegrate the modern, instrumental reason of the sciences into the larger experiential nexus of wisdom, of *sophia* and *phronēsis,* that we may know what can be done and what is better left undone.

The project of Western, scientific-technological civilization has become the destiny of humankind. We can neither continue as before without bringing about universal catastrophes, nor withdraw from this larger project and allow the world to come to ruin without us. Our only option is a thorough reformation of the modern world. Hence, let us reinvent the modern world!

Is there still time? We do not know, nor are we permitted to know. If we knew that our time were already up, we would do nothing more because there would be no point. If we knew that we still had a great deal of time, we would also do nothing, leaving all our unsolved problems to coming generations. But because we do not know whether and how much time yet remains, we must act today as if the future of all humankind depended on us, and yet at the same time trust that God will remain loyal to his own creation, and will not let it fall.

Christianity and the Revaluation of the Values of Modernity and of the Western World

JÜRGEN MOLTMANN

In this essay, I do not intend to defend the "values" of the Western world in the feared "clash of civilizations" (Huntingdon) against representatives of Islamic "theocracies" (Iran) or Confucian "educational dictatorships" (Singapore). Neither do I intend to reinforce the Western "feeling of self-worth," nor consider the status of that self-worth. Modernity and the Western world must come to terms with their crises of values on their own. Every defense against external attacks merely hinders the "revaluation of values" that must take place today in the West if humankind and the earth are to survive. Rather, as a Christian theologian I intend to ask: What do modernity and the Western world owe to Christianity and to the biblical traditions that have entered into them largely through Christianity itself, and what in Christianity and in the biblical traditions is a burden to them? By "biblical traditions" I am also referring to Judaism, to which the modern, Western world owes more than it realizes. I am referring above all to that particular shaping of the Western world by the "Old Testament," by Abraham's exodus, by the God of Israel, by the so-called politics of Moses, and by the

23

visions of the prophets. The inspiration of the Western world by biblical traditions extends even into the fundamental notions and fundamental values of modernity; the Western world has redis-covered its own history of freedom in the biblical story of God and has identified with that story even in secular figures. However, ever since we discovered the "dialectic of the Enlightenment" (Adorno and Horkheimer) and have been suffering under the internal con-tradictions of modernity, it may well be that a postmodern world will take leave of these biblical impulses just as it takes leave of modern impulses, and will do so precisely because it identifies the latter with the former. As Christian theologians, we must thus ask ourselves whether and how from the perspective of our own tradi-tions and hopes we, too, might participate in overcoming the in-ternal contradictions of modernity that we — or our predecessors — have obviously caused. The values of society and their revaluation represent original tasks of public, Christian theology. From the perspective of its origins and its goal, Christian theology is *public* theology, for it is the theology of the *kingdom of God.* Its historical traditions relate the "history of the future," and its prophetic tradi-tions outline the visions of this future. What do these traditions say in our present crises of values?

1. The God of the Bible and the Experience of Reality as History

There is a correspondence between a given regard for values and the experience of reality. So let us begin with the biblical "experience of history" (Georg Picht) and inquire concerning the values of human beings as persons and of human fellowship.

The God about which the biblical traditions speak is not already revealed in the laws and cycles of nature, but rather is revealed through the decisions of human beings and in contingent events of human history. This is why God is named after the human beings whom he has called and after the events through which he has revealed himself to human beings. There is the "God of Abraham, Isaac, and Jacob," and the "Father of Jesus Christ." There is "the Lord" who liberated his people Israel from the historical power of Egypt, and there is "the Father" who liberated Christ from the power of history, from death. The God of historical callings and of saving experiences is justifiably called the "God of history" in contradistinction to the gods of nature.

Judaism, Christianity, and Islam, all of whom appeal to the God of Abraham and to the life experience of Abraham, understand themselves each in its own way as "historical religions." For them, historical recollection is just as constitutive as future expectation. Every comparison with the great Asiatic religions of the cosmos demonstrates the uniqueness of the Abrahamite religions: The future is something new, and is not the recurrence of the past. The world does not exist within the great balance of the cosmos and its harmony, but rather as God's creation it is directed toward the future of his kingdom, and for that reason it is temporal. The "arrow of time" governs all systems of material and life that are in a state of evolution. In the process of tradition and innovation, time is not reversible but rather irreversible, and is experienced in the difference between past and future. The past is irretrievable reality, the future is open possibility, and the present is the interface at which the possibilities of the future are either actualized or missed, and thus at which the future is mediated with the past. The "Abrahamite religions" discovered and sanctified not space but rather time. Elsewhere, the divine was venerated in the ever-recurring order of the cosmos, whereas here it is encountered in the element of the new introduced by the future.

This understanding of reality, described but briefly here as the time of history, has a special affinity with the modern understanding of reality, since the modern world emerged from the extraction of

human culture from its correspondences and concordances with
nature. The agricultural world was superseded by the industrial
world, the village by Megalopolis, and Megalopolis by Technopolis.
Through industrialization and urbanization, a human world
emerged that is constructed solely according to human wishes and
standards, a world through which alone the values of human beings
are actualized. In modern, mass cities, cities that in a few years will
be the domicile and home of more than half of all humankind, the
sun is replaced by neon lights, and meadows and forests by streets
and roads. This city needs neither plants nor animals, living rather
from its own creations. The real world perceived through the senses
is simulated and eclipsed by the "virtual reality" of the computer
and the information superhighway. As a result of orders issued in
Brussels just this week, the older standards of inches, yards, and
miles — standards actually acquired from the proportions of the
human body — have been replaced even in England by the metric
system of centimeters, meters, and kilometers. Increasingly, the natural environment of human beings is being replaced by a technical
environment, and the natural landscape by the "media landscape."
The course of every individual life is no longer determined by the
cycles of the earth and the rhythms of the celestial bodies, but rather
exclusively by the tempo of the modern world itself. Although we
will have occasion to investigate this in greater detail as it involves
the self-experience of the inhabitants of the modern world, it is
enough at this point to note that this extraction of human culture
from the earth itself has generated that particular "ecological crisis"
that can condemn to failure the entire enterprise of modernity.
Environmental destruction grows proportionally according to the
urbanization of human beings, as demonstrated by the increasing
need for energy and the production of refuse in big cities. If Christian theology has introduced into the modern world this understanding of reality as "history" and thus the displacement of nature
and its subjugation, then it is both its self-critical and cultural-critical

task to develop values for a reconciliation with nature and a new harmony — one capable of survival — between modern culture and nature. "Progress" is the leitmotif of modernity; "equilibrium" was the leitmotif of premodern cultures. What we need for survival is a balance between "progress" and "equilibrium" — that is, if we are to develop from the older cultures of equilibrium and from the modern culture of progress the *ecological culture* that will be the culture of the twenty-first century.

Is the God of the Bible really as one-sidedly and in as modern a fashion the "God of history" as modern theology has asserted? Is he not from the very outset — and not merely retrospectively — believed to be the "Creator of heaven and earth," and his creative wisdom venerated in the laws and cycles of nature? A good example of a one-sided reading of the biblical traditions is the famous *Old Testament Theology* by my teacher Gerhard von Rad, who maintained that with its "God of history" Israel supplanted the fertility cults of Canaan, "historicized" the cyclical annual festivals through recollections of its own redemptive history, and thus "secularized" nature.[1] At the end of his life, however, he discovered "Israel's wisdom" and corrected himself.[2]

With what did Israel replace the fertility cults in the land of Canaan? By no means with a notion of pure worldliness for the sake of using the land, but rather with "the sabbath of the earth," commensurate with the creation story (Lev. 25 and 26). In the sabbatical year and in the year of jubilee, fields are to remain unsown so that the earth can pause and "observe a sabbath for the Lord," this 'fallow period making it possible for the exploited earth to regenerate itself. In the sabbath legislation for human beings, animals, and the earth, the great difference between the biblical "God

---

1. Gerhard von Rad, *Old Testament Theology*, 2 vols. (New York: Harper & Row, 1962-65).

2. Gerhard von Rad, *Wisdom in Israel* (Nashville: Abingdon, 1972).

of history" and the modern experience of history becomes clear. The sabbath is also the characteristic sign for the distinction between the world as "nature" (perpetual fertility) and as "creation" (with the interruptions of sabbath rest). We thus find that in the biblical traditions the "God of history" is no other than the "Creator of heaven and earth," and that accordingly the "experience of history" remains surrounded and embedded in the experience of nature. If we intend to address the question of the values and life experiences of modern human beings, then we can do so only with an integrated model of *history in nature*.

2. The Human Being: Part of Nature or a Person?

Whereas all Asiatic and African religions understand human beings as part of nature, the biblical traditions introduced into the world the understanding of the individual human being as a person. Human beings understand themselves to be *part of nature* when they believe that the earth is their "mother," the moon their "grand-mother," and that their lives are "floating" in the great "family" of all living beings in the cycles and rhythms of the sun, moon, and earth. Human beings understand themselves to be part of nature when they believe in reincarnation, because every individual living being comes from within the great weave of life and then returns into it — in order to come back again in other life forms. Finally, individual human beings understand themselves to be part of nature when they understand themselves to be merely members within a long series of generations. Family members that precede them are ancestors to be venerated; family members that come after them are the children for whom they work. The individual consciousness understands itself to be embedded in and carried by the collective consciousness. The death of individuals is of no great significance, since the progression of generations remains, as shown by the generational lists in the Old Testament and, for example, in Korea. The "Earth Charter" of the United Nations Organization (Oct. 28, 1982) thus calls human beings "part of nature."

By contrast, every modern declaration concerning human rights begins with a fundamental article about the inviolable "dignity of human beings." But in what does this unique "dignity of human beings" consist? It is the dignity of every individual human being for himself or herself, and presupposes the individuality of each and every human being. This individual human dignity is the source of all individual human rights, as established in the Universal Declaration of Human Rights of 1948 and signed by all the member nations of the United Nations. Personal rights, equal rights, as well as the freedom of faith, conscience, opinion, and assembly all follow from the notion of individual human dignity. How is this human dignity protected? By insisting that no human being may be treated as an object, but rather always and everywhere is to be respected as a subject. Any reduction of human beings to slaves, to mere labor, or to merchandise — as in the case of prostitution — is thus prohibited. The modern democratization of politics begins with this principle, namely, that "all human beings are created *free and equal.*" All liberation movements and liberation theologies work on the basis of this principle. No one may be disadvantaged because of a handicap. The statement "the patient is a person" applies to all humane medicine. We do not need to describe these consequences further, since everyone is familiar with them.

The modern understanding of the dignity of each and every human being derives from the biblical traditions and from the history of their influence in the Western world. They are concerned, however, with the individual human being not as an "individual," but rather as a "person." An individual, like an atom, is literally that ultimate element of indivisibility. An ultimate element of indivisibility, however, has no relationships, and also cannot communicate. Hence Goethe is quite correct in his dictum: *"Individuum est in-*

effabile." If one has no relationships, then one also has no characteristics and no name. One is unrecognizable, and does not even know oneself. By contrast, a person is the individual human being in the resonant field of the relationships of I-you-we, I-myself, I-it. Within this network of relationships, the person becomes the subject of giving and taking, hearing and doing, experiencing and touching, perceiving and responding.

In the theological sense, the "person" emerges through the call of God, who calls human beings out of their relationships in their homeland (Gen. 12:1). Abraham and Sarah, who follow the call of God and set forth, are the prototypes of the biblical person. So also does God call Moses "by name," and Moses steps forth and says: "Here I am" (Exod. 3:4). The prophets are called after his model, and according to Isaiah 43:1 the following applies to everyone: "Do not fear, for I have redeemed you; I have called you by name, you are mine." That particular God who is not part of nature, but rather who stands independently over against nature as creator, brings it about that human beings, in his image and in correspondence to him, step out in a fashion that juxtaposes them both with the visible creation and with themselves (Ps. 8). Human beings become persons before God on earth. This makes their lives singular and incapable of repetition. It elevates them above other creatures with relative freedom and bestows upon them a special commission in the name of that transcendent God, yet also burdens them with special responsibility for other living creatures. Put theologically: The *dominum terrae* commission of human beings follows from the *imago Dei* structure of what it means to be human. According to the biblical traditions, the dignity of human beings consists in their being created in the image of God. Pico della Mirandola introduced this into the Renaissance culture of the Western world in his famous treatise *De dignitate hominis* (1486), thus preparing the way both for the acknowledgment of human rights and for occidental anthropocentrism. The consequences, both positive and negative, have been profound. Here are two of these positive and negative values.

1. *Abraham's, Sarah's, and Hagar's children.* If human beings are persons, called out of the world by the transcendent God, then they lead an Abrahamic existence. They leave their familiar environment of family, home, and homeland, and become strangers in a strange land. They feel at home nowhere until their hope in God's promise is fulfilled. Although this freedom is transcending the world, it is the freedom of the wilderness. Abraham's children are characterized by openness to the world on the one hand, and by homelessness on the other. The present never gives them rest or entices them to linger. As long as the divine promise is not fulfilled, their hearts remain restless. In both good and bad, they become *bestia rerum novarum cupidissima;* dissatisfied with all their surroundings, they break through all barriers. Their impulses are immoderate because they have been stimulated by the infinite God. But if Abraham becomes the "father in faith" of the Jews, the Christians, and the Muslims, and if Sarah and Hagar always go along rather than stay at home like Penelope in Homer's story of Odysseus, then the corresponding cultures will be characterized not only by dominion over nature but also by alienation from nature. Nature cannot be the "mother" of someone who, like Abraham and Sarah, follows the God of promise. But then what *is* nature for the children of Abraham and Sarah?

As Paul explains in chapter 8 of his letter to the Romans, nature becomes in a positive sense the "sister" and traveling companion of hoping, searching human beings. It is not only human beings who live from hope and yearn for the redemption of the body from the dominion of death. All other earthly creatures and even the earth itself also groan under the power of transitoriness, and yearn for the glory that the "children of God" are already experiencing in their freedom. It is God's Spirit itself that groans within believers as well as in all transitory creatures for the new world of eternal life, and that reveals the sufferings of this time to be the labor pains of that eternal home of all things. That is, the *restless world* corresponds to the *restless hearts* of the children of Abraham. All transitory creatures are, along with Abraham's children, on the way to that future in which the *restless God* comes to rest and finds his home in the house of the completed creation. There, too, Abraham's children find the home of their own identity. All creatures are traveling companions of the children of Abraham, who harbor a profound understanding with all other creatures. They do not view the world as being divided into cosmos and chaos, but rather as a process moving in a unified fashion toward its redemption.

2. *Augustine's lonely soul.* The inhabitants of the Western world are both blessed and burdened by Augustine's soul, since no one has shaped occidental psychology more, and no one has more profoundly grounded Western individualism, than this Latin church father. He desired to know "God and the soul." "And nothing else? No, nothing else." But why precisely and only the soul? Because the human soul bears the image of God within itself like a mirror. Thus whoever would know God must forget the world, close off all the senses, and enter into oneself through meditation; then one will simultaneously recognize both self and God. "Go back into yourself: truth dwells in the inner person." For Aristotle, the soul was one human organ among others. He could describe objectively the characteristics of the soul. For Augustine, however, the soul became the inner self of a person, mysterious and unfathomable. Through his reflexive inwardness, along whose paths he sought both God in himself and himself in God, Augustine discovered human subjectivity. Descartes, with his own philosophy of modern subjectivity, merely followed him, adopting Augustine's own argument: I can doubt all sense impressions, but not the fact that it is I who am doubting; I can deceive myself in all things, but not in the fact that it is I who am deceiving myself. The inner certainty of self is stronger than any external objective certainty, for it is immediate, whereas

the former is merely mediated through the senses. Put simply: Each person is his or her closest, most intimate referent, for we know ourselves best. This is why love of self is the presupposition for love of one's neighbor, and only love of self leads to love of God. If the soul is the subjectivity of the ego, then it governs the body and the senses and is not governed by them. Here, too, the soul corresponds to God: If God is the ruler of the world, so also does the soul as correspondent to God rule the body. The likeness of God in human beings comes to expression in self-governing and self-control, as Puritanism and Pietism have taught the modern world.

But Augustine erred when he considered that this likeness of God inhered only in the soul of the individual human being. "So God created humankind in his image, in the image of God he created them; male and female he created them" (Gen. 1:27). The likeness of God is to be found in the mutual relationship between man and woman, and this relationship is always mediated through the senses and through the body. There is no biblical reference to any precedence being accorded to the self-reflective individual soul. One does not find God by going into oneself, but rather by going out of oneself. The whole human person is the likeness of God in the unity of soul and body, of the internal and the external, of the spirit and the five senses. The entire human community of women and men, parents and children, is to correspond to God and become his reflection on earth. The differentiated unity of person and nature corresponds to God's idea of creation: The person represents nature, and nature sustains the person. Burdened with "Augustine's soul," we today are searching for the "return of the body" and the "redis- covery of the senses" and of the world perceived through the senses, and in so doing we are listening to feminist theology.

The separation of person and nature is mortally dangerous, and leads to moral irresponsibility. Radical humanism, such as that advocated by Peter Singer, defines the human person as the subject of knowledge and will. Human beings who are not yet, no longer, or have never been in control of their knowledge and their will are viewed not as human persons, but rather only as "human material." Such include embryos and fetuses, the severely handicapped, and the senile aged. In reality, however, only the healthy person between the ages of thirty and fifty is a person in the full sense. Prior to this, one is a person to be developed, and after this one is a pensioned person. It follows, then, that only a "person" in the full sense of the word has claims to human rights, while "human material" can be treated like an object of nature. This radical humanism thus leads to perfect inhumanity, since it withdraws human dignity from life that is allegedly "not worth living."

Theologically, the likeness of God inherent in human beings is grounded not in their qualities, but rather in their relationship with God. This relationship between human beings and God is of a twofold nature: It is God's relationship with human beings, and it is the relationship of human beings with God. The objective likeness of God inherent in human beings consists in God's relationship with them, and this relationship can be neither destroyed nor lost. Only God himself can suspend it. The dignity of each and every human being is grounded in this objective likeness of God. God stands in a relationship with every embryo, every severely handicapped person, every aged senile person, and is respected and honored in them when their dignity is respected. Without the fear of God, his likeness is not respected in every human being, and then reverence for life is lost because it is displaced by the perspective of utility. In the fear of God there is no life that is "not worth living."

3. The Person between Personal Freedom and Social Loyalty

In traditional societies, an individual person's entire life was predetermined and regulated from the cradle to the grave. *Membership* in families, castes, social strata, and a particular people determined the course of a person's life, with little room for personal decisions and development. One's personal name meant little, and in some societies daughters were simply numbered, since after their regulated marriage they acquired the family name of the husband. By contrast, one's family name meant everything. A "good family" insured one's social status. One had to come "from a good house," as we used to say in Germany. In traditional societies, stability meant everything, while individuality meant little.

Modern societies place the values of personal freedom above the values of membership and belonging. Tradition no longer shapes life. We live in *free-choice societies,* for we believe that only in its individual persons can a society become creative. This is why we may no longer accept anything as predetermined and prearranged. Every person must be able to determine everything himself or herself: free choice of school, vocation, partner, domicile, politics, religion, and so on. We are even working on being able to determine freely our genetic composition as well. Nothing is permitted to be "fate," not even gender; everything must be determinable. In semi-traditional societies in Europe, a person is yet addressed by the family name; in completely modern societies, and among young people, the only name that applies is Jim or Joan, that is, a person's first or individual name.

Modern big cities individualize and isolate persons. Only in villages or smaller towns can one live in an extended family. Modern apartments and cars are designed for at most four persons — father, mother, and two children. Free choice of vocation and free choice of domicile are tearing the older extended families apart. Ever since our own children have been living in Berlin, Hamburg, and New York, we rarely see our grandchildren. In the big cities of Berlin, Hamburg, Frankfurt, and Munich today, more than half of all households are single households. More and more, family members are becoming single persons. This does not necessarily mean isolation, though this too is present to an unnerving degree, for example, among the aged; to a much higher degree than before, freely chosen friendships are replacing the predetermined family. The residential group *(Wohngemeinschaft)* is becoming the new life form, and "patchwork families" are emerging in which no one knows or cares anymore just who is descended from whom or who is related to whom, but rather only who cohabits with whom or who is living with whom. "Parental substitutes" are replacing relatives.

In every living room, the public sphere is furnished by television. Although every person is indeed merely sitting alone in front of the television set, such persons do participate in all the events of the city, nation, and world, or at least they think that this is the case, even if in truth they are participating merely in the "virtual world" of previously selected information and entertainment. Certainly, a person can turn the television on and off, but this act does not constitute control of the media. Although people can indeed participate in everything insofar as they watch the news, they cannot participate in determining these things, since they cannot broadcast anything themselves. This distinguishes the television public from every human discussion. Human beings are always rendered controllable through individualization: *Divide et impera.*

Finally, there are indications that a new *culture of death* is emerging. In traditional societies, a person was in a religious sense "gathered to his fathers" and in an earthly sense interred in the family grave. In the cult of ancestors, in the Korean Chosuk festival, and at the Christian All Souls' Day or *Totensonntag*, people visit and decorate the graves of their ancestors. In modern societies, personal care of graves is becoming increasingly difficult because people no longer live in the vicinity of the cemeteries. Religious interest in the family tradition is disappearing. This is why there are more and more "anonymous burials" in the secular spheres of modern human beings: the corpse is cremated and the ashes spread on a field or in the sea. "No one knows the place. . . ." The isolated, now merely self-determinative person disappears into nothingness. Actually, this is quite consistent, since the family name already counted for nothing in life. Why should it now bind the children to the graves of the dead?

A series of excellent attempts has been made to balance out the deficits of the human person in modern society through a reflection on the values of the traditional society. I am referring not to conservative and fundamentalist retrogressions, but rather to the *communitarian* idea of strengthening once again the sensibility of modern human beings for the notion of membership and belonging. This includes the creation of local forms of community in overseeable circumstances, a reacquisition of the values of the common good and an enhanced appreciation of social consensus, the development of a participatory economic democracy — all in all: the idea of the "good society," of a "civil society," actualized at every level, both large and small.

I agree with such a balance between the values of personalism and communitarianism, and will contribute no further vision here, but rather will restrict my considerations to the freedom of persons, a freedom that as a result of ever-progressing individualism cannot be maintained. Neither can it be surrendered for the sake of belonging to a traditional society. In my opinion, it can be preserved only through dependability and loyalty. The free human being is "the being that can promise" (Friedrich Nietzsche) and that must also *keep* these promises. Through promises that I make, I in my ambiguities am making myself unequivocal both for others and for myself. In the act of promising, a person defines himself or herself and becomes reliable, acquires fixed contours, and can be addressed. In keeping one's promises, a person acquires identity within time, since that person reminds herself of herself whenever she is reminded of her promises. It is only within the nexus of promises and fulfillment of promises that the free person, the person not predetermined by traditions, first acquires continuity within time and thus identity.

A person who forgets his promises forgets himself; a person who remains true to his promises remains true to himself. If we keep our promises, then we gain trust; if we break our promises, we are mistrusted — we lose our identity and no longer know ourselves. This identity of the human person within a life history is designated by that person's name. Through my name, I identify myself with the person I was in the past, and anticipate myself as the person I want to be in the future. I can be addressed by my name; I sign contracts with my name and vouch for my promises. Free persons live together socially in a dense weave of promises made and kept, of agreements and trustworthiness; such coexistence cannot exist without trust. It is not predetermined *membership,* but rather *covenant* that is the paradigm of a free society; and this covenant is based on social consensus.

The making and keeping of promises, the giving and receiving of trust — these are not restrictions on personal freedom, but rather the concrete actualizations of that freedom. Where do I feel personally free? In a supermarket where I can buy whatever I want, but where no one knows me and not even the cashier looks into my eyes? Or in a community in which I am accepted, and in which others know and thus affirm me as I am? The first is the reality of individual freedom of choice, the second the reality of communicative freedom. The first focuses on things, the second on persons. For me, true freedom is realized through mutual acknowledgment and reciprocal acceptance; that is, it is realized personally through friendship, and politically through covenant.

4. The Modern Distress of Time and the "Discovery of Slowness"

Modern human beings are everywhere and always at a loss for time. Has the Christian understanding of irreversible time and of the incessant march of time from the future into the past brought us into this temporal distress? How can we be relieved of this distress? Never before have human beings had as much free time as today, and never yet have they had as little time. Time has also become "valuable," since "time is money." Although the world offers us unlimited possibilities, our own lifespans are short. Hence many people panic because they think they might miss something, and thus they accelerate the tempo of their lives. The difference between our lifespan and the world's possibilities seduces us into a "race with time." We want to gain more time so we can get more from life, and precisely in so doing we miss life. We believe that only the person who lives faster gets more out of this short life. What we so proudly call "our modern world" is called such because we are forced to modernize it at an ever faster pace. We move increasingly quickly from one place to the next, collecting so many "experiences" in experiential parks like Disneyland or on experiential vacations that sociologists now speak about our "experiential society" (Gerhard Schulze, *Die Erlebnisgesellschaft,* 1993). We make more and more "contacts" with other people, and we know many people. "Fast food" has become the symbol of our "fast life."

The modern *homo accelerandus* is cared for by McDonald's: poor guy! He has a great many encounters, but does not really experience anything, since although he wants to see everything, he internalizes nothing and reflects upon nothing. He has a great many contacts, but no relationships, since he is unable to linger because he is always "in a hurry." He devours "fast food," preferably while standing, because he is no longer able to enjoy anything; after all, a person needs time for enjoyment, and time is precisely what he does not have. Modern people have no time because they are always trying to "gain more time." Because a person cannot essentially prolong her life, she must hurry so that she can "get as much as possible from life." Modern people "take their own lives" in the double sense of the word. By seizing it this violently, they kill it. The scarcity of time is not diminished by a single second through accelerated living; quite the contrary, because of the fear of coming up short and missing something, a person does indeed come up short and misses everything.

We tourists have been everywhere, but we have arrived nowhere. We always only had time for a brief visit. The more we travel and the more quickly we race after time, all the more meager do the spoils become. We are everywhere in transit, and only in transit. A person who lives ever faster so as not to miss anything always lives superficially and misses the deeper experiences of life. Everything is possible in that person's world, but only very little is real.

The mechanical time of omnipresent clocks governs our lives. The clock is the key machine of the industrial age. "You have the clock, we have time," said an Indian guru to a friend of mine. Such time does not care whether the measure of time was empty or full, whether boredom desolated us or whether "time flew": after sixty minutes, the hour is gone. Mechanical time pays no attention to our experienced time, and makes all times the same. Experienced time, however, is the quality of our lives; measured time is merely its quantity. "Happiness is aware of neither the hour nor the minute," we say. Hence it is important in times of intensive life experience to put aside one's clock, or at least no longer to pay attention to it. Life becomes enlivened only when we break this dictate of the clock.

It is presumably our own repressed fear of death that makes us so hungry for life. Our individualized consciousness tells us: "Death is the end of everything; you cannot keep anything and you cannot take anything with you." Unconscious fear of death manifests itself in accelerated haste in life. In traditional societies, individual persons understood themselves to be members of a greater whole such as the family, life as such, or the cosmos. Even if the individual dies, that in which that individual participated does, after all, go on living. The modern, individualized consciousness, however, knows only itself, relates everything to itself, and thus believes that with its own death "everything is over." Perhaps we cannot return again to the old sense that we "belong" to a greater whole that endures even when we pass away. We can, however, surrender our own finite and limited life to the eternal, divine life, and then receive it back again from that divine life, just as this happens in the experience of the community of God in faith. The experience of the presence of the eternal God brings our own temporal life as if into an ocean that surrounds and supports us when we swim in it. Thus does the divine presence surround us on all sides (Ps. 139) like a broad space of life that not even finite death can restrict. Within this divine presence, we can affirm our limited life and become engaged in its limits. We become calm and composed, and we begin to live slowly and with enjoyment. Only the person who lives slowly gets more from life! Only the person who eats and drinks slowly, eats and drinks with enjoyment: slow food, slow life! *The Discovery of Slowness* by Stan Nadolny has justifiably become a bestseller and a consolation for overstressed modern souls. Only the person who is extremely rich can waste time. A person who is certain of eternal life has a great deal of time. We linger then in the moment, and open ourselves up to the intensive experience of life. We experience eternity in the moment *(Augenblick)* that is lived utterly and completely. Is not the life intensity of the experienced moment more than any hastening, in the extensive sense, through one's time of life?! Only repressed fear of death makes us hungry for life and in a hurry. The experienced proximity of death, however, teaches us to experience utterly and intensively every single moment as an eternal moment. This proximity sharpens our own senses in unimagined ways. We see colors, hear sounds, and taste and feel as never before. The experience of death that we accept makes us smart for living and wise in dealing with time. The resurrection hope that we seize opens up a broad horizon beyond death, so that we are able to take time for ourselves.

In the meantime, industrialists in some branches of our economy became aware of the stagnation caused by the so-called acceleration trap and they changed from short-term to long-term products. The costs of developing new technologies and ever new products are growing so fast that one can gain profits only when they become long-selling items on the market. If the time span to sell them becomes shorter and shorter, the profits become smaller and smaller, and in the end they fall below the development costs. This is the "acceleration trap." Only the change to long-term products leads out of this trap. This is possible if you do not sell the whole product anymore but only the use of it, that is, "leasing." Maintenance and repair sustain the long-term life of the product. There are, for example, already laser printers for computers that function without limits. There are already long-term cars. "Waste-making" products are no longer "modern." The longer a car can be used, the more manual labor and local garages become necessary. Long-term products serve labor and the environment, because they use less energy and raw material. Cheap cars use much energy and raw material and produce more waste and unemploy more people, because they can be produced by robotics. The "discovery of slow-ness" today is significant for the ecological reinvention of modern industry and is highly relevant for humans and nature.[3]

How much more is this true for human beings! Is "life in the fast lane" humane and worth living? Some employees prefer a lower income and more free time to a time-consuming manager position; some managers give up their ninety-hours-a-week job in order to live a "good life" instead of having more and more. Many of us are looking for a new attitude toward life and a new lifestyle that allow us to rest in ourselves and escape from the terrors of calendars and their "timing" of everything. We may need a new spirituality of

---

3. Cf. W. Stahel, *Die Beschleunigungsfalle oder der Triumph der Schildkröte* (Stuttgart: 1995).

calmness and relaxation, in order to differentiate between important and unimportant things and to pay better attention to ourselves and our families. If we do not just want to "use," to "consume," or to "spend" our limited lifetime, but to really live our lives, it is good for us to discover the dimension of eternity again, as that which remains in the ups and downs of life and does not vanish.

In conclusion: The modern world has emerged from the Western world, even if one no longer really sees that this is the case, for example, in Asia. The Western world emerged from Christianity, especially Protestantism. Human rights and personal freedoms such as freedom of religion, of beliefs, and of conscience, the democratic political forms and the liberal understanding of life — all these emerged together with Protestantism. The crisis of values of modernity and of the Western world is also a crisis of Protestantism. We are thus called in a special sense to work toward the necessary revaluation of values so that this world may live rather than die.

Theology for Christ's Church and the Kingdom of God in Modern Society

JÜRGEN MOLTMANN

1. From the Confessionally Unified State to a Multireligious Society

Colleagues from other disciplines occasionally ask whether theology really does belong at a modern state university;[1] after all, the university is there for all who want — and who also are able — to pursue a higher education, while Christian theology is there only for Christians, who in fact represent only a minority within modern society. Why, then, do we not simply withdraw and remain among ourselves in church seminaries? Does Christian theology have a task transcending the church itself, a task in the public arena of modern society? The change within modern society itself, one to which the above subheading alludes, has rendered the position of Christian theology so uncertain that it must be discovered anew. What we

---

1. In Germany we have state universities with theological faculties, either Protestant or Catholic. A "university" is a unity of various faculties, a *universitas litterarium,* not just a set of professional schools.

45

have seen thus far in this regard, however, represents only tentative attempts.

The various stages of social change can be quickly delineated:

1. Constantine's conversion turned the Christian minority — which had been persecuted and merely tolerated — into the state religion for the unity of the Roman Empire: one emperor, one law, one empire, one religion. Faculties of theology could be found at state universities beginning in the thirteenth century, and the designation *facultas theologica* was first used at the University of Paris.

2. After the Reformation, the Western split in the church continued the notion of the confessionally unified state: *Cuius regio — eius religio* was the peace formula of the Augsburg and Westphalian treaties. For each state that meant: one ruler, one church, one university, one faculty of theology, either Protestant or Catholic. The eighteenth century gave rise on the one hand to absolutistic states that expelled their religious minorities (Huguenots, Salzburg peasants, Reformed Hungarians) because they believed in *un roi, une loi, une foi,* and on the other hand to confessionally tolerant states such as England, Holland, and Prussia that accepted both Protestant and Catholic churches and theological faculties next to one another. Since 1817 my own university in Tübingen has had both Protestant and Catholic faculties.

3. What happens, however, when immigration causes confessionally mixed Christian states to become multireligious societies? In that case, religion can no longer be state religion. The separation of church and state must open up the way for many different religious communities. Yet if the state itself becomes religiously neutral, then religions must become apolitical. *Beside the point*

Until now, three responses to this new situation have been possible:

1. The faculties of theology at state universities (*theologische Fakultäten*) remain in place, and continue to represent the religious status of the state, which is now multireligious. Dogmatic theology is then changed into the "empirical study of faith and worldviews,"

as at the Swedish University of Uppsala. Or Christian theology is changed into a post-Christian "pluralistic theology of religions," as propagated in the United States by John Hick and Paul Knitter.

2. The faculties of theology remain in place, but now implement — in addition to a Christian course of study — additional courses of study for Islamic, Jewish, and Buddhist believers, or for whatever religious faiths happen to be present in sufficient numbers, as at Cambridge in England. This, however, turns the older faculties of theology and venerable divinity schools into modern departments of religious studies. These various courses of study do not need any spiritual connective.

3. Specifically theological training reverts to the Christian churches themselves, who establish their own theological seminaries for this purpose and no longer concern themselves with university studies. Their own courses of study and exams no longer require any university standard or certification. At the present time in Germany, various atheists and fundamentalists, and some Catholic bishops, have entered into an unholy alliance for the sake of sundering the faculties of theology into religious studies *(Religionswissenschaft)* on the one hand, and ecclesiastical studies *(Kirchliche Wissenschaft)* on the other. One group wants to get rid of theology, the other wants to get control of it.

The only argument militating for maintaining the faculties of theology at our universities is that of tradition, namely: Before we became a multireligious society, we were a Christian country. Only within Christianity is this modern society possible, a society that separates religion and state and guarantees religious freedom. The secularized state lives from such presuppositions, presuppositions it cannot itself guarantee. Although this argument from tradition is indeed venerable, it becomes ever weaker over time.[2]

---

2. Similar problems with faculties of theology or divinity schools as hitherto described occurred in privately founded "Christian universities" in the United States.

Protestant theology after the First World War prepared the way
for this development: "Theology is a function of the church," stated
the unanimous declaration of the "new" theologians Barth, Brunner,
Bultmann, Tillich, and others against what they criticized as "cultural Protestantism" and "liberal theology" after the collapse of
bourgeois culture in the First World War. At the same time, conservative bishops such as Otto Dibelius in Germany proclaimed "the
century of the church" (1925), and abandoned culture to its own
crises. But if theology is only "a function of the church," then it
must leave the university and withdraw from this public arena into
its own community of faith within church seminaries, where it will
submit to the church's own teaching office (magisterium), either the
"infallible Bible" or the "infallible" teaching office of the pope.
Although one might try to maintain a certain independence for
theology by distinguishing between theology and ecclesiastical
leadership, such that the one side variously reminds the other of its
real task, this can hardly be implemented in practice if theology has
no real institutional independence from such church leadership. In
Germany, this development has resulted in a reduction of what is
Christian to the church, and of the church itself to the official
church, because churches are revolving around themselves and no
longer consider other people capable of independent theological
insight.

The separation of religion and state is the presupposition for
any modern society, and this is precisely why fundamentalists of
all religions attack it so vehemently. In many Western countries,
this has led to the misunderstanding that religion is thus no longer
a matter of the state, but rather a "private matter" left to the
individual as an individual freedom. The arbitrariness of religious
decisions is well suited to the individualistic trend within modern
society. Religious pluralism has become a constituent part of the
offerings of the free market of modern society. But who is to shape
what is common and shared within this modern, pluralistic society,

that is, its requisite legal and moral framework? There can be no religious pluralism without certain common foundations, just as there can also be no multicultural society without a common language.

Just what is left over for the state after such separation from church and religion depends on the particular church or religion from which this state has separated:

1. In the English-speaking countries and in Germany, the result was a pro-religious neutrality of the government toward religion and *positive religious freedom.* The religious freedom mentioned in Article 4 of the German Constitution is guaranteed according to the preamble to the constitution by "our responsibility before God." In the United States, the separation of church and state grew out of the principle of independent Christian churches and the restriction of the government from church affairs.

2. In France, the revolution of 1789 was accompanied by an areligious neutrality toward religion and by the guarantee of *negative religious freedom,* since here as also in Italy and Spain an anticlerical laicism fought for and gained religious freedom as freedom from the clerics of the church.

3. In the Orthodox east European states, the socialist separation of church and state resulted in the utterly un-Marxist establishment of Marxism as a substitution for religion and in an *atheistic state religion.* After the collapse of Marxist ideology, Orthodoxy once again occupied the position of popular and state religion.

If religion as a "matter of the state" is made into a "private matter," it is then unavoidably reduced to the private sphere. It then can be lived only privately and no longer publicly. It must be lived in a purely spiritual fashion and may no longer be lived politically. Its symbols and rituals must disappear from public life, as have crucifixes from Bavarian schools and prayer from American schools. It must be restricted to worship of God and to a person's own, personal lifestyle. This means Christianity without the Sermon on the Mount, Judaism without Torah, and Islam without *shari'ah.*

The presupposition of this privatization of religion is that religion be depoliticized, and the result is that religion is then *merchandised.* What we call the modern, "multireligious," and "multicultural" society is actually nothing more than the total and global market society. Religions and cultures are put on sale at the marketplace, just as are moral options and political parties. Religions become the spiritual service that is offered in the religious supermarket of the modern world. Although individual religious freedom does indeed represent strong protection for the personal human dignity of every person, it has turned religion itself into merchandise whose customer is allegedly the "king." The marketing of religions gives them the characteristics of merchandise: They are put on sale arbitrarily and with no obligation and at a discount as "religion light," like the merchandise in *esoterica* sections of bookstores. Everything is possible; nothing is real. Why, really, should a person have a relationship with one religion only, that is, have a monogamous religious relationship? How can I become "multireligious"? Japan has the "three-religion" movement, Taiwan the "five-religion" movement. From each religion people take only what they need and what tastes good, but without any commitment.

This path has led from religion as the "first duty of every citizen" to "religion as a private matter" to "religion as merchandise." Although one can indeed assert that "without peace between the world religions there will be no world peace" (Hans Küng), in reality world peace is attained through politically shutting down, privatizing, and merchandising religions — that is, not through recognizing them but through reducing them to nonentities. One need not be a fundamentalist to view this as atheism in practice.

2. Theology of the Kingdom of God for Christ's Sake

Christ proclaimed the kingdom of God, and what came was the church — these are the words of the well-known Catholic modernist Alfred Loisy. However, he is expressing not only an element of disappointment here, since the church is no substitute for the yet outstanding kingdom of God, but also its anticipation under the conditions of history. If according to its own self-understanding, however, the church is a form of the kingdom of God in the history of this world alienated from God, then it is always concerned with more than just the church itself. In the proclamation of the gospel, in the fellowship of faith, and in the service of love it is concerned with the *world in the kingdom of God* and with the *kingdom of God in the world.* God's future, symbolically designated as the "kingdom of God," includes the future of the world: the future of the nations, of humankind, of all living creatures, and of the earth on which and from which everything lives that is here. The "kingdom of God" is the most comprehensive horizon of hope within the biblical writings for the history of the world.

If the church represents a historical form of the coming kingdom of God, then theology cannot be merely a "function of the church" and cannot restrict itself to offering a Christian "doctrine of faith" (Friedrich Schleiermacher), "church dogmatics" (Karl Barth), or the "grammar of faith" (George Lindbeck). If theology takes the church seriously, then it — like the church itself — must become a function of the kingdom of God in the world. And as a function of the kingdom of God, theology also belongs in the political, cultural, educational, economic, and ecological spheres of life within society. This can be seen in political theology and in the theology of culture, in ecological theology and in the theology of nature. In each of these spheres, the theology of the kingdom of God is public theology that participates in the *res publica* of society and "gets involved" both critically and prophetically because it views public matters from the perspective of the coming kingdom of God. Of course, in so doing it also subjects itself to public criticism, something church memoranda and papal encyclicals notoriously avoid. The theology of the kingdom of God is *theologia publica*, public recollection of God, grievance against God, and hope in God. As public theology, Christian theology is relatively independent of the church itself, since in addition to its ecclesiastical mandate it also has political, cultural, economic, and ecological mandates (Dietrich Bonhoeffer). To that end, it needs institutional independence over against the church, as, for example, in the theological faculties at state universities.

One example: The fifth postulate of the Barmen Declaration of the Confessing Church in opposition to Hitler declared: "It [the church] recalls God's kingdom, God's commandment and righteousness, and thus the responsibility of the rulers and the ruled." The horizon of the kingdom of God is important here, since the assertion is not that the church reminds the government of the interests of the church as fixed in ecclesiastical contracts and concordats. According to the Barmen Declaration, the church is not representing itself over against the state but rather is representing something universal: God's kingdom and righteousness.

Is religion a "private matter"? "Religion" may be, but not the Christian faith. Christ did not proclaim any private religion, but rather the kingdom of God. For the sake of the coming kingdom of God that he proclaimed to the poor and sick in Israel, he was publicly crucified in the name of the Roman Empire as a rebel, as attested by the inscription on the cross. Christian martyrs from Stephen to Dietrich Bonhoeffer and Oscar Arnulfo Romero all went to their death for the kingdom of God. Within the Roman Empire, Christianity could have survived unchallenged as a private religion, a domestic religion, or a religious association, since this multireligious and multicultural empire of Rome was quite tolerant. Through the Christian martyrs, however, Christianity refused to accept the cult of the emperor, a cult necessary for the unity of the empire itself and one that transcended religions and cultures; in so doing, Christianity became politically dangerous. A person who does not become engaged publicly for the kingdom of God has no need to go underground into the catacombs.

Which public sphere is addressed by the theology of the kingdom of God? If we return to Christ's own proclamation of the kingdom of God, we see clearly that the kingdom of God is focused especially on the poor, the sick, and the weak of any given society, as demonstrated by the Beatitudes of the Sermon on the Mount. For the sake of Christ, every Christian theology of the kingdom of God will become a theology of liberation for the poor, the sick, the sad, and the outcast. So the theology of the kingdom of God does not concern itself just with the present public sphere of its society formed by "the rich and the famous," but rather tries to bring into the light of that public sphere those particular persons who in a given society have been pushed into the underground or into the private sphere. It brings the eschatological light of the coming redemption into the present public sphere and discloses the human need for redemption.

The *separation of church and state* does not mean that religion must become a private matter and that the church must become something restricted to private associations. Religious freedom means not only personal choice of religion but also the freedom of ecclesiastical institutions and of Christian establishments: Kindergartens, schools, universities, newspapers, television, educational and service institutions all introduce into society the universal concern with the kingdom of God as entertained by the church in its own freedom from the state. Even in a multireligious society, the church's task is to bring the gospel, faith, and love to all people. Not only individual, private persons but also societies themselves are the addressees of the church's message of the kingdom of God. No church that appeals to Christ and hopes in the kingdom of God can do without this "public character" of that which it represents; to do so would be to give itself up. And this by no means involves any sort of "ecclesialization" of the world. It is not the church that has "something to say" about every single problem, and not the pope, either. At issue is rather an orientation of all the spheres of life toward the coming kingdom of God and toward an alteration of those spheres commensurate with that kingdom. Here, "laypersons" have something to say as Christian specialists. All the spheres of life contain conditions that contradict the kingdom of God and his righteousness, and conditions that correspond to it. It is these correspondences under the conditions of history that are at issue. A determined Christian minority representing universal concerns can attain this more effectively than can an immobile Christian majority.[3]

What are these universal concerns today, concerns that allow no pluralism and no arbitrariness? Today, life itself is in mortal danger. Since Hiroshima in 1945, humankind as a whole has become mortal. We are living in a secular end time, that is, in a time in which the nuclear end of humankind can happen at any moment. Tens of thousands of nuclear weapons are available for this "final solution" to the question of humankind. There will be no time now in which humankind can forget the formulae of its own self-annihilation. The consequences of this for the church of the kingdom of God are that it must pursue unconditional service for the sake of peace

3. Is there a contradiction between my "kingdom-of-God perspective" and Nicholas Wolterstorff's "Christian learning"? I do not see one. We agree on three points. First, if there is a "general priesthood of all believers" then there is also a *general theology* of all believers. Whoever believes and thinks is a theologian, not only the professionals, whose task is to serve and train Christians. Second, there is no such thing as "Christian mathematics," "Catholic biology," or "German physics." *Christian learning* can bring only the universal aspects of the kingdom of God into the sciences, not the particular aspects of Christian faith. Third, the significance of a faculty of theology in a university is, in my view, to keep the question of truth (*die Wahrheitsfrage*) present in the other faculties, so that they may not become professional schools only; and to fight for and preserve the freedom of the sciences over against state ideologies and market interests.

and must work to eliminate war as a solution to conflict. The consequence of this for the theology of the kingdom of God is a consistent theology of peace. According to biblical traditions, the "kingdom of God" means shalom, peace on earth. Humankind is supposed to live, since God is a God of life. As we know, there are no other reasons for the survival of humankind.

Life itself is in mortal danger. Since Chernobyl in 1986, we know that contamination can render entire regions uninhabitable for centuries. The consequences of this for the church of the kingdom of God is a "reverence for life" (Albert Schweitzer) and a fellowship with the earth and with all living creatures. For the theology of the kingdom of God, the development of a new ecological theology becomes unavoidable. For the anticipated kingdom of God encompasses both human beings and the earth; without a redemption of the earth itself, there will be no salvation for human beings.

Life itself is in mortal danger. Overpopulation has resulted in more and more "surplus" people being born, people no one wants and no one needs. Crimes against this allegedly "surplus" life are just as much a part of the crimes of the modern world as are the crimes against nature and the potential crimes against humanity wrought by "devices of mass annihilation." Abortion of unborn lives, abandonment of street children, unemployment of both women and men, premature death as a result of the return of epidemics — these are only a few of the crimes against life today. The consequence of this for the church of the kingdom of God is an unqualified engagement on behalf of life. For the theology of the kingdom of God, the development of a "theology of life" becomes important. God's Spirit is the "source of life" *(fons vitae)* and the "vivifying spirit" *(spiritus vivificans)*. The future of the kingdom of God in this dying world begins with the presence of this Spirit, and hope in this kingdom is grounded in the experience of the Spirit that vivifies. In the pluralism of the various religions and cultures in modern societies, the church with its theology of the kingdom of God will represent universal hope for life amid the common dangers threatening humankind and will invite other religions and cultures to work together in overcoming these dangers.

3. The Kingdom of God and the Fellowship of the Church with Israel

The fact that the basic scripture of Christianity consists in the duality of the Old and New Testaments represents something special and unique within religious history. Other religions, such as Judaism, Islam, and Buddhism, have unified basic scriptures. Closer examination reveals that the basic scripture of Christianity consists in the Tanakh of Israel and the gospel of Christ: there "the law and the prophets," here the "gospel and the apostles." According to Martin Buber, the church shares with Israel "one book and one hope." The book is the Tanakh/Old Testament, the hope is hope in the kingdom of God. Hope in that future in which God's glory will fill all lands (Isa. 6), and in which God will make all of creation into his dwelling place *(miškān)* (Rev. 21), does indeed reduce the promissory history of Israel and the history of Christ and of the Spirit to a common denominator. This hope runs like a red thread through the scriptures both of Israel and of Christendom. In this context, however, the Old Testament cannot be integrated into the New Testament as its preliminary stage, nor can the New Testament be reduced to a commentary on the Old. The designations "old" and "new" are misleading, since in actual practice the church reads the two Testaments next to one another, not one behind the other, and prays the Psalms along with Israel. Like Israel, Christendom prays for the hallowing of the name, the doing of the will, and the coming of the kingdom of God, as the Lord's Prayer attests.

Out of this duality of the two Testaments there emerged for

Christians a hope in the kingdom of God, since only in the eternal kingdom will the hopes of Israel and of the church be fulfilled. The "promissory surplus" of the Old Testament extends beyond the coming of Christ and of the Spirit, and directs both toward God's future. The theology of the kingdom of God formulates the "future of the scripture" of the Old and New Testaments, and thus also their unity. The search for a "center of scripture" that began with the Reformation, when "scripture" became the teacher of the church and of theology, cannot be successful, since every center presupposes a complete circle, while the scriptures of the Old and New Testaments do not constitute such a "self-enclosed system," but rather are witnesses that disclose the future, and as such are thus historical witnesses. The biblical traditions are historical insofar as they, as it were, point "ec-centrically" beyond themselves into that particular future of God in which "scripture is fulfilled." They tell the story of that particular future called the "kingdom of God." The kingdom of God thus becomes the guiding notion of every "biblical theology" that not only reads the Old Testament in light of the New and the New Testament in light of the Old, but also takes seriously the fact that the "Old Testament" of the Christians is at the same time the Tanakh of Israel. This means that the theology of the kingdom of God in its complete scope and depth can be developed only in productive cooperation between Jews and Christians, between the church and Israel. In this process, neither Christians nor Jews will level their abiding differences, but rather will make full creative use of them. If both sides were to say the same thing, one would be superfluous.

Within the horizon of this hope in the kingdom of God, the church realizes that it is not the only form and anticipation of the eternal kingdom within the history of this world. It acknowledges Israel as an earlier and as a simultaneous anticipation of the kingdom that Jesus proclaimed, a kingdom God began with the resurrection of Christ and the pouring out of the Spirit. This means that the substance of the kingdom of God is not only shaped in a Christian fashion, but must also be understood in a Jewish fashion. One sign of this is the apocalyptic visions of the Revelation to John: According to chapter 7, those who are saved include those "sealed out of every tribe of the people of Israel" and "a great multitude that no one could count, from every nation, from all tribes and peoples and languages." According to chapter 21, the gates of the city of God will be named after the twelve tribes of Israel, and its walls after the twelve apostles of the church.

In the history of this unredeemed world, Israel and the church remain distinct: The future of Israel is not the church, and the future of the church is not Israel. The church should not try to Christianize Israel, nor can it devolve into Israel. Israel and the church, each in its own way, witness to the nations God's kingdom, righteousness, and peace. For with Israel, the electing God's concern is not Israel; and with the church, his concern is not the church. Rather, with both of them God is concerned with the redemption of the nations and of the earth into his eternal kingdom. For a long time, the distinction between the church and Israel was an oppressive element for Jews in the Christian empire; and ultimately, in the "thousand-year *Reich*" of the political pseudomessiah Hitler, it became deadly. In view of the shared scriptures and the connecting hope in the kingdom of God, however, this distinction can also be extremely fruitful — at least for the church.

4. The Mission of Life in Relation to Other Religions

There are two kinds of dialogue between religions: direct and indirect. *Direct dialogue* is religious dialogue among what are known as the "world religions," that is, religions not bound to a single culture and a single people, but oriented rather toward all people and every individual. For this reason, they are found all over the world. These include the three Abrahamic religions, namely, Judaism, Christianity, and Islam, and the Asiatic high religions *(Hochreligions)*, Hinduism, Buddhism, Jainism, Confucianism, and Taoism. Earlier, these religions were also called "high religions" over against primitive nature religions. Even today, the so-called nature religions are not part of the global programs of dialogue. The idea that the world religions might conclude peace with one another and contribute to world peace through an internal "dialogue" is actually a Western idea, since the so-called religions of the Book are naturally better equipped for such dialogue than are meditative religions or ritual religions. The expression "dialogue" is presumably appropriate, since the path is already supposed to be the goal. Nothing more comes from such direct dialogue among representatives of the world religions than better information about one's partner, and an understanding for the differences of the others and respect for one another; no mixing is intended, though mutual influence is probably one result.

Indirect dialogue takes place today at "Earth Day," at Global Forums, and at ecological conferences. Here the issue is the present, mortal dangers threatening humankind of the sort I described earlier, and thus the question is: Which energies can these religions mobilize to avert these dangers? What have the world religions done to destroy this world, and what can they do to save it? Where within these religions do we find life-negating and world-destructive forces, and how can these be changed into life-affirming, world-preserving forces? The ecological crisis threatening the world demands ecological reformations within all the so-called high and world religions, since until now these have had little to say at those conferences, while the despised, primitive "nature religions" are full of insight into the cycles and rhythms of this earth. Although their ancient wisdom is indeed preindustrial, it will become relevant again in the postindustrial age. It is less a matter today of the world religions than of the religion of the earth. Whereas African religions are hardly represented in the interreligious dialogues of the world religions, they become the leaders at ecological conferences.

For direct religious dialogue among the world religions, one can use a "pluralistic theology of religion"; such a theory, however, is actually a metatheory and cannot be called "theology" if it also is to encompass religions without God, such as Buddhism. One has no need of such a metatheory for indirect, ecological dialogue, for which a shared acknowledgment of the mortal dangers at issue enables partners to work toward thwarting such threats and toward providing mutual help in undertaking the religious reformation necessary for insuring that the world may live instead of go to ruin.

It is from this perspective that the meaning of the *Christian mission* within the present world situation comes into view. A new initiative seems to be necessary here, because (a) so far nobody has become a Christian through interreligious dialogue, and (b) the known dialogue programs seem to be nothing more than conservative consolidations of the religious status quo. We have hitherto been familiar with Christian mission as an expansion of the Christian domain: Salvation resides in subjection to the holy dominion of the Christian emperor. Hence during the Middle Ages, the Saxons and Slavs were "missioned" in Europe; in the sixteenth century, it was the Indians in the Americas; and in the nineteenth century, the Africans in Africa. We are familiar with Christian mission as the spread of Christian churches *(plantatio ecclesiae)*: Salvation resides in submission to the teaching office of the church. We are familiar with mission work as evangelization, the awakening of personal experiences and decisions of faith among others. These forms of Christian mission take as their point of departure the particular that is already at hand, and then try to globalize it.

If by contrast we take as our point of departure the kingdom of God, we are beginning with the universal future of the nations and of this earth, which we then try to evoke or actualize it among them. In this case, the emergence of independent and postdenominational churches is embraced rather than lamented. The religions and cultures of other peoples are not destroyed but rather are opened up to God's future and filled with the spirit of hope.

In its original theological sense, mission is *missio Dei.* If our Christian mission follows and is commensurate with the divine mission, it is a mission accompanied by trust in God and by the certainty of faith. If we follow and are commensurate with the divine mission to other people, we resist the temptation to rule over them religiously, and respect their human dignity as the image of God. *Missio Dei* is nothing less than the Father's sending of the vivifying Spirit into this world through the Son. The Gospel of John expresses quite simply just what God brings into this world through Christ: *life* (John 14:19) whole life, shared life, indestructible, eternal life. Jesus did not bring a new religion into the world, but rather *new life.* What follows from this for the mission of Christians is the rebirth of life, arising from the proclamation of God's love for life. Anyone whom God views with the "radiant countenance" of his love is enlivened from the inside out and experiences a new, unconditional affirmation of life. But the rebirth of life also arises from the healing of the sick, the acceptance of the outcast, the forgiveness of sins, the healing of fretful memories — that is, it arises from the rescue of threatened, damaged life from the powers of destruction.

The mission of life does not simply come without presuppositions, but rather becomes engaged wherever there is life and wherever that life is threatened. Indestructible, eternal life, which the divine, vivifying Spirit bestows, is not a life different from this life here, but rather is the power through which this life here becomes different. This perishable, temporal life comes to participate in eternal, divine life (1 Cor. 15:53), becoming thereby indestructible. The "redemptive economy" of the Holy Spirit encompasses all of life and the life common to all that lives; and for that reason, it may not be reduced to religion or to inwardness.

In this context, it is not a question of whether other religions can also be "paths to salvation," or whether people in religions other than Christianity can also seek and possibly find God, or whether there can be "anonymous Christians" also among the members of other religious communities — or whatever the questions may be that address the theological significance of other religions. Rather, in this context it is a question of life itself within those other religions, and similarly a question of life within the nonreligious, secular world. *Missio Dei* means inviting all religious and all non-religious persons to life, to an affirmation and guardianship of life. Anything that in other religions and cultures serves life in this sense is good, and must be appropriated into the "culture of life." Anything that hinders, destroys, or sacrifices life is bad, and must be overcome as the "barbarism of death." God's vivifying Spirit here is the beginning of the redemptive kingdom of God there.

I do not believe that the theological locus at which the plurality of religions must be discussed is the doctrine of original sin, as was earlier the case, nor is it the doctrine of the revelation of the divine truth, as is today the case. For me, this locus is *pneumatology,* and within pneumatology the doctrine of the *multiplicity of charismata.* For this is where the concrete question arises: Can a different religion or parts of it become the charisma of God's Spirit for a person if that person becomes a Christian? What must a person give up when becoming a Christian? According to the earlier classification of other religions into the doctrine of original sin, this person must undergo a radical separation from superstition and from idolatry when becoming a Christian. According to the new, pluralistic theology of religion, such people do not even need to become Christians at all if they have found the divine truth in their own religions. Paul apparently declared everything that a person is, and everything that shapes a person personally, culturally, and religiously, to be that person's charisma at this calling: "Was anyone at the time of his call already circumcised? Let him not seek to remove the marks of circumcision. Was anyone at the time of his call uncircumcised? Let him not seek circumcision. Circumcision is nothing, and uncircumcision is nothing; but obeying the commandments of God is everything. Let each of you remain in the condition in which you were called" (1 Cor. 7:18-20). Accordingly, with divine right there are both "Jewish Christians" and "Gentile Christians." The keeping of God's commandments in the freedom of Christ becomes the criterion for what can and cannot become charisma, that is, for what can and cannot be engaged as power and service in the witness of faith. Jews must not become Gentiles, and Gentiles must not become Jews when they become Christians. For the Jewish Christians of that time this is understandable; but what does it mean for "Gentile Christians"? They are not simply "non-Jews" but come rather from their various cultures and religions, which they bring along with them even if they leave their gods behind. Early Christianity was not shy about making full positive use of whatever they brought along from their "Gentile" religions; rather, it openly embraced anything that was good, just, and beautiful. The Church in Rome *Maria supra Minerva* shows graphically how the Roman cult of Minerva was appropriated into the Christian veneration of Mary. Even today, the festivals of the ecclesiastical year still correspond in our own culture to the annual Germanic festivals of Christmas, Easter, and Pentecost. Although one might condemn this as "syncretism," it is better to view this as the charismatic adoption of other religions and as an engagement of their life forms in the service of the kingdom of God. Charisma is anything I can put into the service of building up the congregation and anything I can engage for the kingdom of God. Christianity does not occur in this world in a naked and pure form. If, then, there is a Roman, Germanic, and Slavic Christianity, why not then also a nonreligious Christianity as well, and a Hindu, Buddhist, and Confucian Christianity? If the goal is not the church itself, but rather the kingdom of God, then anything commensurate with the righteousness and life of God can be taken along on this journey. Hence one can discover in other religions perspectives on the kingdom of God, on eternal life, and on the new earth, all of which are important for Christianity just as they are important for those other religions.

Let me conclude this essay with a small vision relating to church history. We can — as was also the case earlier — divide the history of the church into three epochs:

1. The age of *primitive Christianity*, its mission, and its expansion, extends from the apostolic beginnings up to the "Constantine turn" in the Roman Empire.

2. With Constantine's conversion there began that particular epoch of Christianity associated with *the state church and the popular church*. This was associated with the "Holy Empire," the "Christian World," and is viewed in Europe and the United States as "the Age of Christianity."

3. In Europe and America today, we are entering a "post-Christian age," that is, in actuality a "post-Constantinian age." Christian faith is no longer represented in the world by the spread of the *Corpus-Christianum* Christianity and by its division into confessions and denominations throughout the world. Everywhere, postdenominational, independent churches, Pentecostal churches, are emerging — churches that no longer derive from European traditions but rather from the influence of the Holy Spirit. They might be a premonitory sign that we are now living in the *age of the Holy Spirit* and have the kingdom of God before us.

Public Theology or Christian Learning?

NICHOLAS WOLTERSTORFF

1

Theology, to be genuinely Christian, must be kingdom-of-God theology. Kingdom-of-God theology is inherently *public theology*. And the proper sponsor in the modern world for public theology is the public university. Those are the central theses in Jürgen Moltmann's essay, "Theology for Christ's Church and the Kingdom of God in Modern Society." Let me begin by laying out, in brief compass, how Professor Moltmann develops these theses.

I take Professor Moltmann to assume — the assumption is unspoken — that theology properly conducted is not some neutral, generically human, enterprise, but comes in what one might call "confessional" forms. There is Jewish theology, Christian theology, Muslim theology, and so forth. Christian theology is the theological articulation of the Christian gospel; normally it will be practiced by those who themselves embrace that gospel. We can expect that when the kingdom of God is fully realized, the distinctions among Judaism, Christianity, Islam, Buddhism, and so forth will melt away, as the consequence of our coming to see clearly what now we see darkly. But in the meantime, we live with these distinctions; and part of how we live with them is that each religion has its own theologians and its own theology. I do not hear Moltmann urging his fellow theologians to ignore such distinctions — to rise above them or dig beneath them so as to practice some sort of generic theology: natural theology, foundational theology, common-denominator theology, or some such thing. Neither do I read Moltmann as himself attempting any such theology. Moltmann sees himself as a *Christian* theologian.

But the gospel that the Christian theologian articulates is not a message just for Christians. Nor is it a message just about the ecclesiastical and devotional side of our human existence — about church life and devotional practices. The Christian gospel is the gospel of *the kingdom of God.* It speaks of the coming of God's reign, of signs and samples of that coming, of hindrances to its coming, of the mode of life appropriate to its coming. It speaks of the divine lament and the divine delight. And the Christian theologian, along with every Christian, shares in that lament and that delight. "We are theologians because in the face of this world we miss God," says Moltmann; I have no doubt that he would add that we are theologians as well because here and there in this world we find God. But what we lament is not only deficiencies in the ecclesiastical and devotional lives of human beings. We lament the absence of justice and righteousness in society; we lament the injuries wreaked upon earth and our fellow creatures; we lament the anguish and restlessness of the human soul. In short, we lament the absence of "life," as Moltmann calls it. Thus "for me," says Moltmann, "theology . . . springs from God's *love for life,* the love for life that we experience in the presence of the life-giving Spirit, and that enables us to move beyond our resignation, and begin to love life here and now."

That is the *content* of the Christian gospel, and hence of Christian theology: Christian theology is kingdom-of-God theology. Accordingly, Christian theology is addressed not just to Christians, not just to the church, but to all human beings. Its *addressees* are all human beings. To each and every one of them it speaks of the kingdom of God. To all of them it speaks of the divine love for life, and of the divine lament over the destruction of life.

Since its addressees are each and every human being, Christian and non-Christian alike, Christian theology must be public theology. That is to say, its *arena* must be the public space. That is where the theologian's voice must be heard. In the church too, of course. But since the *content* of Christian theology goes far beyond church and devotional life to life as a whole, and since its *addressees* extend far beyond church members to humanity in general, its *arena* must be civil society. "As kingdom-of-God theology, theology has to be public theology: the public, critical, and prophetic speech of God — the public, critical, and prophetic hope for God. Its public character is constitutive for theology, for the sake of the kingdom of God." Since its proper arena is the public space, its institutional *sponsor* ought to be those public institutions of civil society that support and promote scholarship — preeminently, the public university. "Public theology needs institutional liberty in relation to the church, and a place in the open house of scholarship and the sciences." In summary: since kingdom-of-God theology addresses all human beings concerning all spheres of life, its arena must be the public space of civil society, and it ought to be maintained by the public institutions of civil society. Let me say that, with all this, I resonate deeply.

Moltmann goes on to observe that today, however, the presence of Christian theology in the public university is endangered. Endangered especially, as Moltmann sees it, by an unholy alliance of atheists and fundamentalists — meaning by the latter those who, because they regard the content of Christian theology as the church, likewise want its arena and its sponsor to be the church. "Today the dissolution of theology into a science of religion on the one hand,

and the churchifying of theology on the other, are driving theologians out of the university. And in this attack on the liberty of theology and its public character, atheists and fundamentalists seem to have forged an unholy alliance."

The churchifying of theology, Moltmann suggests, is the consequence of a pair of distinct, but symbiotic, dynamics. There is, on the one hand, the trend in the modern world toward what is often described as the "privatizing" of religion. The "symbols and rituals [of religion are to] disappear from public life, as have crucifixes from Bavarian schools and prayer from American schools. [Religion] must be restricted to worship of God and to a person's own, personal lifestyle. This means: Christianity without the Sermon on the Mount, Judaism without Torah, and Islam without shari'ah." My own view — and Moltmann's also, if I understand him — is that the dynamic which is working itself out here is not really toward the privatizing of religion but rather toward its spiritualizing. The customary description of it as the privatizing of religion is a misdescription. For religion, certainly in the United States, is far from a private phenomenon. American religion is marketplace religion. It is present in the public square, aggressively so — though less in the political than the economic life of that square. In Moltmann's words, "religious pluralism has become a constituent part of the offerings of the free market of modern society. . . . Religions become the spiritual service that is offered in the religious supermarket of the modern world."

The other dynamic that, in Moltmann's view, has contributed to the churchifying of Christian theology is a dynamic within Christian theology itself rather than within Christian life. Moltmann identifies it as the tendency among Christian theologians in the contemporary period to regard theology as merely a "function of the church," restricted "to offering a Christian 'doctrine of faith' (Friedrich Schleiermacher), 'church dogmatics' (Karl Barth), or the 'grammar of faith' (George Lindbeck)."

It will be clear from the foregoing that Moltmann's response to both of these dynamics is his insistence that the content of the gospel that the church is committed to live out, and that its theologians are committed to articulate, is not the church but the kingdom. Christian theology, to say it again, is kingdom-of-God theology. "If theology takes the church seriously, then it — like the church itself — must become a function of the kingdom of God in the world. . . . The theology of the kingdom of God is *theologia publica,* public recollection of God, grievance against God, and hope in God. As public theology, Christian theology is relatively independent of the church itself, since in addition to its ecclesiastical mandate it also has political, cultural, economic, and ecological mandates. To that end, it needs institutional independence over against the church, as, for example, in the theological faculties at state universities."

We are discussing, remember, Moltmann's identification of the dynamics that have endangered the position of Christian theology in the public university, and his response to those dynamics. The dynamic, or rather, pair of dynamics, that we have discussed is that of the churchifying of theology. The other dynamic is the spread of atheism.

Although Moltmann does not say what exactly this second dynamic amounts to, I infer that he thinks of it also as having a dual aspect. One aspect of this dynamic is the charge, coming not only from the atheist but from all who regard academic learning as properly a neutral, objective enterprise, that confessional theology is an anachronism in the public universities of the modern world. Religion and theology, if they belong in the public university at all, belong there only as the subject matter of some *objective* discipline. Confessional enterprises have no place in the public university. The other aspect of this dynamic is the charge, coming not only from atheists but also from representatives of other religions than Christianity, that the maintenance of faculties of Christian theology by public universities violates the fundamental commitment of constitutional democracies to the freedom and equal treatment of all religions and irreligions to be found in society.

It is not clear to me how Moltmann proposes answering these objections. I surmise, however, that his answer to the first of them — the objection that a faculty of confessional theology conflicts with the commitment of the modern university to neutral, objective *Wissenschaft* — I assume that his answer to this objection is contained in the following words of his: "who is to shape what is common and shared within this modern, pluralistic society, that is, its requisite legal and moral framework? There can be no religious pluralism without common foundations, just as there can also be no multicultural society without a common language." In other words, Christian theology provides a service to the citizenry in general; it ought, on that ground, to be maintained by the university. Every society needs a normative basis — "common foundations," in Moltmann's phrase. It is this that Christian theologians provide, by speaking to each and all concerning the demands and hopes of the kingdom of God.

I surmise that Moltmann's answer to the second objection — that a faculty of *confessionally Christian* theology in a public university is incompatible with the fundamental commitment of constitutional democracies to the freedom and equal treatment of all religions to be found in society — I assume that his answer to this objection is contained in what he calls his "pluralistic theory of religion." The idea is that just as Christianity has developed beyond its primitive Jewish form to make room not just for Gentile Christianity as such but for a host of different forms of such — Roman Christianity, Germanic Christianity, Slavic Christianity, and so on — so also it must now develop to make room for Hindu Christianity, Buddhist Christianity, Confucian Christianity, and so on. Perhaps even — Moltmann's thought on the matter is not clear to me — it must make room for atheist Christianity. The issue in each case, as Moltmann sees it, is whether the religion in question promotes "life." The mission intrinsic to Christianity is not the mission of evangelizing for conversion but the "mission of life." "Anything that in other religions and cultures serves life in this sense is good, and must be appropriated into the 'culture of life.' Anything that hinders, destroys, or sacrifices life is bad, and must be overcome as the 'barbarism of death.'" "Although one might condemn this as 'syncretism,'" says Moltmann, "it is better to view this as the charismatic adoption of other religions and as an engagement of their life forms in the service of the kingdom of God." In short, Christianity ought not to be exclusivistic; it ought to "charismatically adopt" whatever in other religions promotes life. And Christian theology, as the articulation of Christianity, ought correspondingly to be syncretistic. If it is, then there is nothing inequitable in the public universities of the modern world maintaining faculties of confessional Christian theology.

2

Thus far, summary. Let me begin my engagement with Moltmann's line of thought with this final point; as I proceed from here, what will gradually emerge is a quite different perspective on the task of Christian theology and its place in society from that which Moltmann offers. Let me at the outset repeat, however, that I too understand the gospel of Jesus Christ as the gospel of the kingdom of God; on this fundamental point, there is complete agreement between us. Our disagreements will be over the implications of that perspective for the task and place of Christian theology in the modern world.

I begin with Moltmann's response to the charge of inequity, of unfairness. I fail to see that Moltmann answers the charge. I fail to see how his proposal concerning the place of confessional Christian theology in the public university is in fact compatible with the commitment of our constitutional democracies to the freedom and equal treatment of all religions in society. His proposal, as I understand it — possibly I *mis*-understand it — is that the theology faculties of the public universities are to remain faculties of *Christian* theology — on the condition that Christian theologians syncretistically absorb into their theology the contributions of other religions, insofar as those serve "life." He is definitely not proposing that theology faculties become faculties of religious studies; nor is he proposing that they become religiously pluralistic. They are to remain faculties of *Christian* theology — on the condition, however, that other religions become adjectival modifiers to the Christian substantive. Thus, for example, Muslim Christian theology, Buddhist Christian theology, Jewish Christian theology, and so forth.

But surely no Muslim, Buddhist, or Jew will regard this proposal as an adequate answer to the charge of unfair hegemony on the part of Christians. No doubt it will also appear religiously arrogant to them. Is it up to Christians whether Islam, Buddhism, and Judaism are to be absorbed into Christianity? Shouldn't Muslims, Buddhists, and Jews have a voice in the matter? But let that pass. The issue directly before us is the charge of unfair hegemony. The Muslim will ask why Islam should be the modifier and Christianity the substantive in the theology sponsored by our public universities. Why not reverse the "grammar," making Islam the substantive and Christianity the modifier?

I assume Moltmann's answer would be that Muslim Christianity is what the gospel of the kingdom of God calls for; it does not call for Christian Islam. And no doubt, when the situation is viewed from the perspective of the Christian gospel, he is right about that. But that is scarcely an impartial view on the situation. The Muslim sees things differently. For one thing, most Muslims call for *conversion,* not for syncretistic incorporation: for the *conversion* of Christians to Islam. Should any grant the legitimacy of syncretism, they would insist that Christianity be assimilated to Islam, not Islam to Christianity. Given this difference of perspective, I fail to see how it is compatible with the commitment of our constitutional democracies to the freedom and equal treatment of all religions for the public universities to grant to Christian theology a hegemonic position within the university. It makes no difference whether Christian theology has absorbed elements of other religions; it makes no difference whether it has been Islamicized, Judaized, or whatever. It remains *Christian* theology. Being such, it is not a theology for all religions. To grant it hegemony in the public university is to violate the equal-treatment principle.

Not only are non-Christians treated inequitably under Moltmann's proposal; so too are most Christians. Only those Christian theologians who embrace what Moltmann calls his "pluralistic theology of religions" are to be granted a place within the university. Why the preference? I surmise Moltmann's answer to be — again, I may be wrong — that a syncretistic theology treats other religions with greater fairness than does an exclusivistic theology. Now it is by no means clear to me that syncretistically assimilating some other religion into my own, when the members of that other do not wish to be assimilated, is a case of treating them fairly. There may be reasons for going forward with such assimilation; I do not see that fairness is a reason for doing so. But be that as it may. There are also many Christians, and many Christian theologians, who reject such syncretism. To exclude them from the university would also violate the requirement of equal treatment. Even if syncretism were the only theologically defensible position, its being such is irrelevant to the commitment of our constitutional democracies to the freedom and equal treatment of all religions. For it is not *correct* religions and *correct* theologies that are to enjoy freedom and equal treatment; it is *all* religions and *all* theologies. If I understand Moltmann's proposal correctly — and let me say, once more, that it may well be that I do not — then he, Jürgen Moltmann, would be allowed to teach theology in the public university, since he is willing to develop a syncretistic theology, whereas Karl Barth would not be allowed to do so, since surely he would not be willing to develop such a theology. That seems to me an unacceptable violation of the principle of equal treatment.

The other objection of the atheist, in addition to the charge that it is inequitable for public universities to maintain faculties of confessional Christian theology, is that it is incompatible with the very idea of the university in the modern world to maintain such. For whereas such faculties are confessional in their orientation, the university is committed to the practice of neutral, objective *Wissenschaft*. Moltmann's answer is that the Christian theology which he is proposing is addressed not just to the church but to everyone; and that it serves the important public service of offering a normative foundation for society. This answer, too, I do not find adequate.

It is not difficult to imagine the response of the atheist: The fact that the theology in question is addressed to everyone is no proof whatsoever that it belongs in the university. Lots of things are addressed to everyone. Theology belongs in the university only if it has been developed by employing the objective methods of the academy. In fact Christian kingdom-of-God theology has not employed such methods. It has employed exegesis of, and reflection upon, sacred scriptures. As to the public service it purportedly performs, of offering a normative foundation for modern society: the offer of a normative foundation for life together made by kingdom-of-God theology is an offer rejected by the atheist, in company with many other members of society. So why should those making that offer enjoy a hegemonic position in the theology faculties of our public universities? Don't the parties making different offers have equal right?

The basic point to recognize and keep in mind here is that Moltmann's syncretistic Christian theology remains confessional theology, and is as much a contested perspective as are the alternatives that he explicitly and implicitly rejects. It is true that it speaks to human beings in general about many dimensions of our existence, and that, accordingly, it seeks a place in the public arena from which to speak. But it does not follow that it has a right to hegemony in the theological faculties of our public universities. It does not even follow that it has a right to be there at all.

3

My engagement up to this point has been negative. Let me now begin the task of reconceiving the situation by isolating and calling into question an assumption that underlies Moltmann's discussion, without ever quite being brought to the surface. The gospel of Jesus Christ is the gospel of the kingdom of God: I agree. Accordingly, Christian theology will be kingdom-of-God theology: I agree. But I do not agree with the apparent assumption *that Christian learning always takes the form of Christian theology.* To assume that it always does take that form represents, from my point of view, illegitimate aggrandizing on the part of theology. "As a function of the kingdom of God," says Moltmann, "theology also belongs in the political, cultural, educational, economic, and ecological spheres of life within society. This can be seen in political theology and in the theology of culture, in ecological theology and in the theology of nature. In each of these spheres, the theology of the kingdom of God is public theology that participates in the *res publica* of society and 'gets involved' both critically and prophetically because it views public matters from the perspective of the coming kingdom of God." Notice the assumption that Christian learning, in these various spheres, takes the form of *theology.* The question I wish to pose is: Why doesn't it take the form of Christian philosophy, and of Christian literary theory, and of Christian political theory, and of Christian ecological theory, and so forth? Is it not also the calling of the

Christian philosopher, and not just the calling of the Christian theologian, to view "matters from the perspective of the coming kingdom of God"? And the calling of the Christian literary theorist, and of the Christian political theorist, and of the Christian ecologist? Are all these spheres of learning to be assigned and consigned to the *civitas mundi,* and only theology to be allowed entry into the *civitas dei?*

At one point Moltmann remarks that "At issue is . . . an orientation of all the spheres of life toward the coming kingdom of God and toward an alteration of those spheres commensurate with that kingdom." To which he then adds that "Here, 'laypersons' have something to say as Christian specialists." But why *laypersons?* Why is the alternative *either* Christian theologians *or* Christian laypersons? Why have Christian philosophers fallen from view? And Christian sociologists? And Christian literary theorists? Moltmann fights valiantly against the spiritualizing of the Christian gospel. I join him in that fight. Yet, as sunset approaches, he lays down his arms before the battle has been finished and tacitly accepts the characteristically modern constriction of Christian learning to Christian theology. I want to propose — indeed, I want to insist — that Christian theology is just one part (an important part, but just one part) of Christian learning.

The picture that unavoidably emerges of the strategy of the kingdom-of-God theology that Moltmann calls for is that theology takes the results of the various academic disciplines, and then performs on those results such activities as setting those results within a larger theological context, pointing out similarities between reality as seen within some nontheological discipline and reality as seen within theology, and so forth. Of course, the theologian will also now and then, here and there, criticize certain of the results. When he does so, he will regularly describe his criticism as "prophetic critique." But to the practitioner within the discipline, these criticisms by the theologian do not usually wear the lofty mien of prophetic critique; they come across as *complaint*. The theologian is a complainer. Those who work within the discipline have been laboring in the hot midday sun. Now, as cool breezes begin to blow, the theologian turns up and complains about what has been accomplished. Why wasn't he working in the field when economics was being developed? Why does he only turn up when the workers rest?

I submit that what the gospel of the kingdom of God, which Moltmann so emphatically calls for, requires within the modern academy is not just *theology* that is kingdom-of-God theology, but learning in all the disciplines that is kingdom-of-God learning, learning pursued in fidelity to the gospel and in the light of the coming kingdom. It is *economists* — *Christian* economists — who will have to work out the import of the gospel of the kingdom for the economic dimension of society. It will not do to consign the development of economics to those who care nothing about the kingdom, and then content ourselves with having theologians around who lodge a criticism here and there against the results and set the totality within a theological context. What is needed is not a theology of economics but theologically faithful economics. I know, of course, that there are many who would say that the Christian gospel gives no guidance whatsoever for scholarship in general, since it speaks of something else than that to which scholars address themselves: of the transcendent, of authentic existence, of spirituality. But note that this is not a reply that anyone who accepts the kingdom-of-God understanding of the Christian gospel would offer.

4

Here is not the place to develop a full-fledged account of Christian learning. But since I can scarcely assume that everyone will understand what I have in mind, I do feel it incumbent on me to offer at least a brief indication. I take it that to be a Christian is, for one thing, to acknowledge God as creator of the universe, and as having dwelt among us in Jesus Christ, and as working within us in the person of the Spirit for the renewal of creation and the instauration of the kingdom. I take it that to be a Christian is, secondly, to participate in the life and work of the church and to make one's membership therein part of one's narrative identity — part of who one is. And I take it that to be a Christian is, thirdly, to accept the Christian scriptures as canonical. Faith of a specific sort, interwoven with identification with a specific community, interwoven with acceptance of specific scriptures as canonical — I take those things to single out Christians from other human beings. Other things as well (Christians carry the mark of baptism), but at least those three things.

To engage in Christian learning, then, is to allow that faith, and that communal identification, and those scriptures to shape one's learning, whatever one's academic discipline. To allow them to shape one's judgments as to what is legitimate to investigate: for example, one's judgment as to whether it is legitimate to engage in research on aborted embryos. To allow them to shape one's judgments as to what is important to investigate: for example, one's judgment as to whether it is important to find out why the disparity between rich and poor in the United States has been increasing over recent decades. To allow them to shape one's convictions as to the conditions that a theory on a certain matter must satisfy if it is to be acceptable: for example, one's convictions as to whether a theory of jurisprudence is acceptable if it works entirely in terms of maximization of utility and not at all in terms of justice and rights. To allow them to shape how one treats one's fellow scholars: for example, one's willingness or unwillingness to speak abusively of men or of women, of whites or of blacks, of conservatives or of liberals — or indeed, of anybody. To allow them to shape how one thinks about faith and church and scripture themselves. And so forth, on and on. To allow the metaphors of the psalmist, Paul's fruits of the Spirit, the parables told by Jesus, the narrative of Christ's resurrection, the pathos for the social outsiders preached and exemplified by the prophets, the prayers of the Eucharist, the philosophy of Anselm and Aquinas, the theology of Bonaventure and Barth, the hymns of Wesley, the etchings of Rembrandt, the poetry of T. S. Eliot — to allow all of these, each in its own way, to shape one's learning, after one has oneself been formed by them. That, I say, is Christian learning. Put it just a bit differently: Christian learning is faithful learning. Learning faithful to the triune God, learning faithful to the Christian community and its tradition, learning faithful to the Christian scriptures.

In addition to that, it is the learning *whereby* one is formed by Christian faith, by the Christian community and its tradition, and by the Christian scriptures. Let me develop just a bit this point about Christian formation and the role of learning therein. Anthropologists in our century have powerfully made the point that, unlike other animals, the biological component in the makeup of us human beings is woefully insufficient for our flourishing — insufficient even for our continuing existence. If we are to survive and flourish we have to be cultured — or better, *en-cultured*. Our difference from the other animals is not, indeed, total; some of them are also not, for example, hardwired with feeding and mating habits, but have to learn them from their seniors. But in the case of us human beings, the cultural programming is vast as compared to the biological hardwiring. There must, indeed, be some hardwiring or we could not even get going in acquiring that programming which consists of our enculturation. Some writers nowadays talk as if everything about us is culture, nothing is nature. I am at a loss to explain how anyone who has given the matter even a moment's thought could think that. If there is no hardwiring inside your computer case, then, no matter what program you try to install, nothing will happen. Yet compared to even the highest of the nonhuman animals, a human being's cultural programming is relatively much more important than one's hardwiring in explaining why one thinks and acts, feels and imagines as one does.

But there is no human culture in general — no human culture *allgemein.* There are only human *cultures.* The enculturation undergone by a member of the Benin tribe in West Africa in the seventeenth century was profoundly different from that which you and I have undergone. Thus it is that there is such a thing as *Christian* culture — or more precisely for my purposes here, Christian *en*culturation. Always a person's Christian enculturation will intersect and interact with other modes of cultural formation: with twentieth-century American modes, twelfth-century Byzantine modes, and so forth. But if to be a Christian is to exhibit a specific sort of faith, to identify with a specific community, and to accept specific scriptures as canonical, then, perforce, whatever else may go into being a Christian, being a Christian will incorporate a certain identifiable cultural formation. And for the acquisition of that formation, education is indispensable. Not necessarily academic learning, but certainly education. In no case will all of such education take the form of academic learning; in the case of some Christians, none of it takes that form. In your and my case, however, very much of it does.

In summary: Christian learning is learning *shaped* by one's Christian formation, and learning which is the *medium* of that formation.

5

What is the proper arena for such learning? The same as the arena that Moltmann regards as appropriate for kingdom-of-God theology: the public space. Christian learning is not just for the church but for humanity in general. It addresses itself to all, and concerns itself with all the diverse aspects of human existence. Its proper arena is the public space of civil society.

We should not, in my judgment, immediately jump from here to the issue of university sponsorship. Civil society in the contemporary world not only offers many other modes for the dissemination of scholarship than the university classroom; it also offers many other types of institutional sponsorship than the university. It may well be that the future of creatively faithful Christian learning in general, and of theology in particular, does not lie in the public universities. It is well to remind ourselves that, until Reid and Kant, almost all of the creative developments in modern philosophy occurred outside the university. Nonetheless, though the university is not indispensable, it is obviously of looming importance in the contemporary world. We cannot avoid eventually considering whether Christian learning has a rightful place in the public university.

Why would it be thought not to have such a place? Because it does not satisfy the conditions, implicit in the project of the modern university, for scholarship that is acceptable within the university. What conditions are those? At bottom, that the scholarship conducted within the university be *generically human* scholarship.

No one is really of the view that, when entering the halls of the university, one ought to deposit at the door all one's beliefs, purposes, and affects. No one supposes that one *could* do that. The idea is rather that one can and should allow the beliefs, purposes, and affects that one has acquired in everyday life to sit in storage, while using, in the academy, only one's indigenous, generically human hardwiring: one's indigenous and generically human perceptual capacities, one's indigenous and generically human rational capacities, one's indigenous and generically human memorial capacities, and so forth. It may well be that some of the beliefs we have acquired in everyday life have not just been deposited in the storehouse of memory but have become components in the programming whereby new beliefs are formed. But it is not in general true that beliefs get formed in us only if we have been suitably programmed. There are, within us, indigenous belief-forming dispositions, belonging to the hardwiring with which every human being is supplied. It is those, so it is said, that must be utilized in the academy. Naturally one must not expect complete consensus on results. But our disagreements will not be grounded in the fact that some of us have been programmed as Christian, some as atheist; some as American, some as German; and so forth.

It is my judgment that the central issue that we must face, in considering whether Christian learning in general, and Christian theology in particular, has a rightful place in the academy, is whether this Enlightenment idea — let's call it that because that is what it is — whether this Enlightenment idea of the academy is tenable. If it is, then Christian learning, be it theological or otherwise, has no place in the modern academy. Its having no place in the academy does not imply, as I observed above, that it has no place in civil society generally. But the very idea of Christian learning is that it is the learning of one whose adherence to the Christian gospel is part of her programming, and who proposes to allow that programming to function in her practice of scholarship; she does not propose trying to circumvent that programming. And that is a paradigmatic example of what is forbidden by the Enlightenment idea. It does not make any difference whether the Christian learning is syncretistic. It does not make any difference whether it is addressed to everyone. It does not make any difference whether it offers normative foundations for society in general. If it is learning that is Christian in the way explained just above, its presence in the academy, given the Enlightenment idea of the academy, is taboo.

Perhaps I should state explicitly here that I am using the words "programming" and "hardwiring" as metaphors. I do not for a minute think that we human beings are in fact computers. Rather, I judge that in computer language we find some words which are helpfully employed as metaphors in trying to state just what it was that the Enlightenment theorists were getting at.

It is my own impression that most of those who have questioned the legitimacy of faculties of Christian theology in the public universities have been working with this Enlightenment idea of the university. I concede that among those who *reject* that idea one also finds some who are hostile to university faculties of Christian theology. The best of their arguments is that such an arrangement is inequitable in our pluralistic societies. The worst of their arguments — though possibly also the most common — is that Christian theologians do not measure up to the requirements for political correctness. But, at least until recently, most of the objectors have been pressing the point that faculties of Christian theology are incompatible with the project of the modern university. Nostalgia may incline us to keep them around for a while; they remind us of the Christian origins of our universities. But sooner or later, they have to go.

Thus it is my own view that it is not an unholy alliance between atheists and religious fundamentalists that constitutes the main threat to the continuance of faculties of Christian theology in the public university. Atheism as such seems to me not now, and never to have been, the basic issue. If theology can be developed in such a way as to satisfy the conditions for membership in the modern university, then it belongs there, whether or not atheists happen to like it. And until well into the twentieth century, most members of the university did in fact think that at least some of it could thus be developed. It is the rise of skepticism on that score that is fueling the present objections. Likewise, the call for "churchifying" theology seems to me not to be the basic issue. Karl Barth, Hans Frei, George Lindbeck — these are no less kingdom-of-God theologians than is Moltmann. They agree that the Christian gospel is not just *about* the church; they agree that the gospel is not just *addressed to* to the church. But they are all vividly aware of the fact that Christian theology, as they think it ought to be practiced, is in conflict with the Enlightenment idea of the university. And it is their conviction that if it comes to the point where the Christian theologian is confronted with the option, *conform to the Enlightenment idea of the university or leave,* the theologian must, with great sadness in his heart, leave.

It would be a deep mistake not to recognize the visionary character of the project of the modern university — the "Enlightenment idea of the university," as I have been calling it. It is the vision of the academy as the place where we set aside all our differences of religion and tradition, nation and class, gender and race, and work together to advance learning. The vision emerged out of the fifteenth- and sixteenth-century wars of religion, when each of the combatants had its own resident theologians and philosophers. And it represented, in a deep way, the continuation of the ancient and medieval project of *scientia.*

Nonetheless, visionary though it be, the idea is unacceptable. It is simply not possible to circumvent the beliefs, the purposes, and the affects acquired in everyday life and make use in scholarship just of one's indigenous, generically human, hardwiring. It is simply not possible thus to circumvent the ways in which we have been programmed by experience, by induction into tradition, and by yet other factors that lead us to "see" things differently from how our fellow scholars see them. It is not possible in our scholarship to circumvent the identities bestowed upon us by our religions, our nations, our genders, our races, our classes. Academic learning is unavoidably perspectival.

I recognize that even with the spread of postmodernism, this contention remains controversial — less controversial than twenty years ago, but not yet the consensus of the academy. On this occasion, I cannot mount a defense. Were I to do so, I would want sharply to distance myself from the typical postmodern embrace of antirealism, and from the accompanying assumption that the academy, at bottom, is nothing else than a shifting constellation of power-blocks. It is of utmost importance that we retain the conviction that there is a structured world out there, created by God, independent of our human activities of conceptualizing and interpreting, along with the conviction that not only does our programming often obstruct access to that reality, but that our nature and programming together also *enable* access. The person who dwells in the underside of society is characteristically thereby enabled to "see" things that the person who lives at the top does not see.

But rather than developing these thoughts further, let me on this occasion simply observe that once it is conceded that learning is unavoidably perspectival, then the preeminent issue confronting us is this: Which forms and modes of perspectival learning are to be allowed into the academy? The old policy was simple: keep them all out. Especially the feminists have persuasively pointed out that what in fact happened was not that the academy was reserved for nonperspectival, generically human learning, but that it was reserved for a narrowly limited range of perspectival learning. Nobody supposes that the new situation should be a free-for-all. If not, then the crucial issue is that of criteria for acceptance. What is urgently needed in our new situation — the situation of shattered illusions — is a fundamentally different understanding of the project of the university from that of the Enlightenment idea, along with a fundamentally different set of conditions for university membership to implement this new understanding. And what you and I, as people who care about the cause of Christian learning, must argue, as we participate in that urgently needed discussion, is that Christian learning, appropriately conducted, has as much right to a place in the academy as Marxist learning, feminist learning, Judaic learning, and so forth.

As much right. Christian learning, and in particular, Christian theology, has as much right to a place in the academy as, for example, Judaic learning. That implies that Judaic studies do indeed have a rightful place in the academy. I am no more in sympathy with turning theology faculties into religious studies departments than is Moltmann. I find Judaism intensely interesting, and Islam. But in religion as such I have no interest whatsoever. Nonetheless, it seems to me clearly incompatible with the commitment of our democratic constitutional societies to the freedom and equal treatment of religion for a public university to limit itself, in its treatment of religion, to maintaining a faculty of *Christian* theology. It makes no difference how ecumenical that theology may be, or how syncretistic. What is called for, instead, is that the religious particularities present in society be honored by the university with a policy of responsible pluralism.

6

Much more begs to be said on all these points. The urgent need of the day is a new theory of the university. But I must close. Let me do so by returning to what, for me, is the central point. I am as persuaded as Moltmann is that the body of Christ must have a voice in the public square, and must use the voice it has. Though rather than saying that it speaks there of *life*, I would prefer to say that it speaks there of *shalom*. It speaks of human flourishing in all dimensions. Let us be under no illusion, however, that we human beings are in agreement as to what constitutes human flourishing. To the contrary, each religion has its own unique angle on human flourishing — on shalom. Thus the body of Christ, though it works to evoke as much agreement as it can, welcoming such agreement wherever and whenever it appears, regards global syncretism as impossible until the day of the kingdom arrives. Buddhism has its own angle on human flourishing; the Christian will honor that angle while disagreeing with it, all the while being open to the possibility that the Buddhist may call to his attention aspects of human flourishing that he as a Christian had overlooked, or even resisted. And vice versa.

If the voice of the body of Christ in the public square is to be anything more and anything other than the loud but hollow voice of aggrieved resentment or wimpy confusion, it needs Christian scholarship. It needs scholarship that holds in memory the long and incredibly rich tradition of Christian reflection while thinking afresh from the perspective of the kingdom of God about art, about the economy, about the polity, about theology. There is a powerful case to be made for opening up the public universities of the modern world to the pursuit of Christian learning, thus understood — given that they are also opened up to other responsible versions of per-spectival learning. It is far more important, however, that Christian learning be practiced *somewhere* than that it be practiced in the public university. The public university, for all we know, may become a thing of the past. It may prove impossible for the university to shed the illusions of generic objectivity of which I spoke without exploding into contentious fragments. Should that prove to be the case, the need for Christian learning would be more, not less. The Christian in the public square will continue to need the Christian scholar to supply her voice with content.

In any case, whatever happens to the public university, the Christian scholar will not cease to find in faithful learning his or her way of rendering thanks to God. I have emphasized the *utility* of Christian learning. Deeper than its utility is the fact that Christian learning is *eucharistic*.

The Crisis of Modernity
and the Christian Self*

ELLEN T. CHARRY

1

Jürgen Moltmann has been the leading voice of our generation
urging theology to stay nimble on its feet. He calls theology to look
outward, to interpret the faith in terms of what is going on in the
world, since the church is called to be an instrument of hope in a
troubled world. In attending to the world the eschatological foundation of Christian faith finds its proper expression. Jesus Christ
confronts the church and the world with fresh possibilities for their
future. Theology, Moltmann has reminded us, is to be an instrument
of hope. As such it is always political activity.

Professor Moltmann interprets Christian teachings dynamically,
offering a reading that supports the most cherished hopes of modernity. His work has encouraged rethinking Christian doctrine away
from a concern with timeless essences and into the living flow of

---

*Note: This essay by Professor Charry responds to a slightly different version
of Professor Moltmann's text than appears in this volume.

history. To this end his early work criticized traditional doctrines that led Christians out of history, such as classical interpretations of the Trinity and eschatology.

The second half of his career brought a new set of organizing concerns. The ecological crisis led Moltmann to see that Christianity's focus on God's presence in history siphoned concern away from nature. He has seen the ecological crisis, the crisis of the cities, and deleterious effects of technology as related to concerns voiced by feminists, black theologians, and other liberation movements. They all unite under the broad general theme of emancipation from domination. In this Moltmann shows himself a true child of the Enlightenment who yet sees contradictions within modernity itself.

In "Christianity and the Revaluation of the Values of Modernity and of the Western World," Moltmann has suggested that modernity must come to terms with its crisis of values on its own; his responsibility is to hold Christian teachings accountable for their complicity in our present ills. Environmental destruction, urban decay, and the psychological damage wrought in late modernity now lead him to criticize the historicality of biblical faith that extracted culture from nature, whereas previously he had cited the abstractness of Christian doctrines. Ever open to new horizons for theology, he now espouses a reclamation of the "experience of nature" suppressed by the biblical witness.

Another problem for late modernity is its conception of the self as individual. This notion tugs at natural bonds of culture and family that once provided a strong sense of belonging. Moltmann sees Christianity as implicated in modern individualism through God's call of Abraham and Moses. He sees the call to step out as creating an individual relationship with an individual God as the norm of personhood and dignity. Augustine picked up on this theme of the "lonely soul" that falls in love with God and leaves the world. Descartes brought this individualism into modernity, so that the internal experience of certainty became the defining characteristic of modern selfhood.

Yet more: rehearsing the old criticism that Augustine never really overcame Manichaeism, Moltmann holds Augustine responsible for alienating us from our bodies and from nature as well as from natural communities. It is only in relationship to God, not in our relationships with one another, that we achieve true personhood. Christian teachings turn out to be ambiguous in the modern context, encouraging attitudes and behavior that undermine traditional forms of community, meaningful relationships, and psychological stability.

Modern alienation and anomie continue to grow apace. Religious and family traditions fall into disuse with increased geographic and social mobility. Community ties are undermined by modern technology. It appears to me, and I may be wrong in this, that the suggestion Moltmann makes to stem the creeping disintegration of modern society is to rely on the individual's ability to make promises and remain dependable and loyal to those promises within the modern identity one constructs for oneself. To be loyal is finally to be true to oneself. Proving to be trustworthy both to ourselves and to others is the actualization of our freedom played out through friendship and political alliances. If I am correct that the themes of promise keeping in friendship and loyalty are Moltmann's main suggestions — again, I may be wrong — it appears to me that the modern self has been reinforced rather than corrected and that Christian theology has been left behind.

While Moltmann locates the source of the crisis of modernity in the crucible of modern individualism, correctly in my view, what is interesting is that he sees this unfortunate theme of modernity as an outgrowth of biblical and patristic themes, without identifying other Christian themes, like self-control as a means to true freedom, that might be used to counteract the deleterious effects of modern individualism. It is only facing death, which seems to propel moderns into frenetic activity and movement, that Moltmann sees the

Christian affirmation of the divine presence offering a note of comfort: "eternity in the moment that is lived utterly and completely." In Moltmann's narrative, Christianity, especially Protestantism, contributes nary more than a whimper to the solution of the crisis of modernity. Perhaps it is simply too tired.

Help, Moltmann argues, is to come not by reclaiming Christian themes that could support communal and familial bonds, but by reinterpreting Christian teachings so that they follow after secular movements, like environmentalism and feminism, that seem to point modern society in a salutary direction. Exactly why a hermeneutic of emancipation is apposite to the environmental and technological crisis is not made clear. Perhaps it is that the dying of the earth and its atmosphere, and the overcrowding of cities with their abject poverty in the Third World, appear to Moltmann as simply another form of hegemonic domination of the powerless by the powerful. If this reading of Moltmann is correct, I beg to disagree. Modern science and economics were created in the name of emancipation and benevolence. If in their maturity science and technology are now revealing unintended negative side effects, calling again for the hermeneutic of emancipation is misplaced. Emancipation is not a one-size-fits-all principle. Sad it is when we need to be emancipated from the means of our emancipation.

As I read Moltmann in this particular essay, his model of the relationship between church and society is culture transforming theology in order to transform culture, to stretch Richard Niebuhr's categories a bit.[1] Would that theology were so powerful. I agree that the West is in self-contradiction and that the individual self is at the core of the problem. I follow Moltmann's lead in believing that Christian teachings must be reinterpreted in order to help. Simply getting the doctrines clear will not do. Perhaps the difference be-

1. H. Richard Niebuhr, *Christ and Culture* (New York: Harper & Brothers, 1951).

tween us is that I now see the hermeneutic of emancipation itself as implicated in the crisis of modernity. While I, too, grieve at the desolation of the earth by modern technology and capitalism, I am no longer persuaded that emancipation — at least in its secular instantiation — is always on the money. What if the crisis of the environment is a *result* of our emancipation — notably our emancipation from God? An indiscriminate use of a hermeneutic of emancipation without any framework for transformation of the self, laid on top of modern individualism, will, I fear, be more problematic than helpful at this point.

I was led to this conclusion by reading patristic literature and seeing that while it too speaks of emancipation it is emancipation from the unlovely side of self that is meant, and that the way to emancipation is through self-mastery achieved by attending to God. Indeed, for the great tradition, proper emancipation requires a critical distance on oneself provided by God and cultivated through discipline and new skills that fit one for a more noble and refined life. Simple emancipation from external authority is insufficient to fit us for the new life required by and for life in Christ. We need God precisely as the one before whom we stand to give us pause in regard to our undertakings. Indeed, it is under the guidance of God that we are transformed and outfitted to confront the crises of our day that are of our own making. In short, to Moltmann's adoption of the secular doctrine of emancipation, I pose a Christian theological understanding of emancipation that is keyed to transformation.

If modernity has spawned the crisis that we see, I believe we must get more distance on modernity than its secular emancipation narrative can provide to see what a viable strategy for addressing it would look like. My own suggestion is to encourage Christians to find critical distance on modernity by rearticulating a basic insight of their own tradition: we need God.

I no longer think that modernity can handle itself, or come to terms with its own crisis, as Moltmann does. Complicity narratives that blame Christianity for modernity's crisis are important, but, I submit, no longer sufficient. They are no longer adequate in part for a psychological reason, and in part because they may claim more than is warranted. The psychological reason may be put as follows. Complicity narratives and the hermeneutic of suspicion currently dominate the theological landscape. Criticism of Christian anti-Judaism, sexism, racism, militarism, the preference for heterosexuality, and so forth render tenderhearted Christians abashed about the content of their faith. This does not encourage Christians to see how the basic Christian claim that we need God might be used to rethink Christian teachings so that they can help in this new situation.

Christian complicity narratives grow out of the norm of self-criticism. In this they may be tempted by reductionism. Christian self-criticism, wanting to show its strength, is tempted to take responsibility for more than its share of problems. It is difficult for me to read modern individualism out of God's call to Abraham and Moses as Moltmann does. On the face of it, Abraham and Moses as well as Augustine were submitting to the will of God, not seeking their fortune. Yet Moltmann has tried to draw a straight line from the Bible through the patristic age to modernity without recognizing critical distinctions between the premodern and the modern mindset. Surely Descartes's teaching on the nature of autonomous reason in the *Meditations,* John Locke's teaching on individual consciousness and his invention of private property, and J. S. Mill's teaching on individualism in *On Liberty* are a far cry from Abraham's and Moses' obedience to God and Augustine's yearning for God.[2]

2. René Descartes, *A Discourse on Method and Meditations on First Philosophy* (Indianapolis: Hackett, 1993); John Locke, *Second Treatise of Government* (Indianapolis: Hackett, 1980); Locke, *An Essay Concerning Human Understanding* (New York: New American Library, 1964); John Stuart Mill, "On Liberty" in *The English Philosophers from Bacon to Mill,* ed. Edwin A. Burtt (New York: Modern Library, 1939), pp. 949-1041.

Complicity narratives, while noble and imperative, must be handled carefully. It may now be tempting to construct an inverted Christian hegemony, taking responsibility for problems beyond Christianity's reasonable reach, and thereby deny the autonomy of other ideas. For example, well-meaning Christians in dialogue with persons from other traditions can interpret non-Christian religious forms and ideas in Christian terms as a gesture of goodwill, only to be met with hostility from the dialogue partner whose self-understanding has been negated. Eagerness to be Christianly self-critical may reach a point of diminishing returns. So, I would claim, it is with the crisis of modern values. The modern values of individuality, autonomy, and freedom that define the modern self may have some distant links to Christian themes, but they now have a life of their own. Even when some terms like "freedom" and "emancipation" are shared they arise from different foundations. The secular self is grounded in itself, while the Christian self is grounded in God.

At the same time, Moltmann is certainly correct that Christianity has shaped Western culture. Yet it is also true that Western values and culture have profoundly shaped Christianity. No doubt Christians have much to account for in every century, because a flawed but guiding principle of the church was that error has no rights. Modern principles of rights, fairness, freedom, tolerance, and equality have taught the church in this regard. Calvin would not be able to execute Servetus now. Today Christians rarely resort to violence against one another concerning matters of doctrine and practice.

While modern values have helped the church restrain itself, my observation, sad to say, is that it is some of those cherished modern beliefs that are today in crisis. I do not come to this conclusion lightly. I myself am a child of modernity who began avidly ingesting secular existentialism and humanistic psychology at age fourteen. Now, of course, I see more than I could see then. I locate the crisis of modernity in a certain secular understanding of the self that disagrees with the Christian tradition on just one small point: that we (really) need God.

In identifying this disagreement between the modern and the Christian self I am not sure whether I offer an alternative to Moltmann's position. All that I can say is that I do not hear this concern expressed in the essay before us ("Christianity and the Revaluation of the Values of Modernity and of the Western World"). This may be an inaccurate judgment, however. Perhaps Moltmann does see a place for a distinctly Christian self in addressing the crisis of modernity. Be that as it may, I am sufficiently persuaded that the secular culture, and to a certain extent Christians themselves, have lost sight of the Christian insistence that we (really) need God and that we can no longer readily envision how a distinctly Christian perspective might be brought to bear on the crises of our day.

While I am grateful that Moltmann has brought the environmental crisis within the purview of Christian theology, my own point of entry into the crisis of the modern self has been through the circumstances of America's youth. I believe the construal of the modern self based on the hermeneutic of secular emancipation is implicated in both problems. But articulating those connections lies beyond the scope of this response. I ask your indulgence in pursuing an assessment of contradictions within the modern self from this particularly North American vantage point.

2

My argument is that the modern self has been constructed around the themes of self-sufficiency and emancipation of a rather shallow sort that fail to take account of the needfulness of the self beyond autonomy and freedom. It is a hermeneutic of release that provides no larger context for transformation and growth. Modern secularism, an ideology first adumbrated by Descartes and Locke, and developed by others, posited a natural self who is not first and foremost God's creature and God's servant, but a free agent, out to seek its fortune in the world. The self, according to Jean-Jacques Rousseau, a chief artisan, is not encumbered by sin and guilt before God. It is good and naturally free, so long as it is not deformed by "civilization." It needs only to be set free from external constraints to flourish, like the female body waiting to be freed from corsets and foot binding. It is also self-sufficient, as Moltmann notes, needing little if anything by way of assistance from outside itself, and owing little to the past or to the community that gave it birth. Its main problem is frustration when things get in its way or it lacks the technology or power to have its way.

Rousseau's educational philosophy, articulated in *Emile,* greatly spurred modern secularism and individualism by grounding education in self-expression and natural development while neglecting self-mastery as essential for social life.[3] His approach to education at the child's own pace and following the child's own interests encouraged resistance to social constraints that inhibit natural self-expression. It is not immediately evident exactly how the theme of emancipation from social influence fits with the social contract designed to counter the possibility of anarchy and provide for the harmonious functioning of modern society. Nineteenth-century Romanticism — starstruck with individuality, personality, and creativity — furthered individual expression as the signal need of the self. This left in the dust the Christian claim that true emancipation requires self-mastery — which is only possible with the help of God and growth in the context of the church.

At the end of the nineteenth century Nietzsche declared God dead. With this the Christian notion of goodness, toward which self-control aims, came under suspicion. In the mid-twentieth cen-

3. Jean-Jacques Rousseau, *Emile* (Rutland, Vt.: Charles E. Tuttle, Everyman's Library, 1974).

tury post-Freudian psychology picked up the hermeneutic of emancipation in psychological terms, adapting the Marxist principle of class struggle to the task of psychological emancipation from family and traditional virtues. Modern poetry, fiction, painting, sculpture, and dance all reinforced the hermeneutic of emancipation on an artistic level, breaking down structures of family, nation, and literary and artistic form all on the assumption that the self contained within itself all that it needed to provide its own happiness.

By the late twentieth century, with the king and God both dead, under the tutelage of poststructuralist critics, all that remains for the self is power, and we cannot even control that. Jacques Derrida has undone the meaning of meaning itself, and Michel Foucault portrays us all as victims of "repressive" modern bureaucracy, whether democratic or Marxist. Today the hypermodern self may be coming into its own, or perhaps to its end, with no limits in sight. An unnuanced hermeneutic of emancipation has reduced society to little more than emancipation's chief demon, the desire to dominate. In the name of inclusivity and freedom the hypermodern self tends toward anarchism. Emancipation, first from external constraint and now from meaning itself, binds this long modern tradition into a single narrative from Descartes to Derrida.

The notion of an autonomous and benevolent self needing emancipation from both internal and external controls overran the basic Christian conviction that we flourish only when transformed by being taken up into the divine life, that one's responsibilities to others are specified by the call and cross of Christ, and that residence in the body of Christ provides an environment for maturation in a worshiping community.

Mid-twentieth-century humanistic psychology from Wilhelm Reich, Erich Fromm, Karen Horney, and Abraham Maslow, to name several important writers, advanced the romantic theme that personal emancipation opposes rather than is assisted by socialization. One chooses what sort of self to become. It may take many years to "find oneself." Indeed, finding, creating, and expressing oneself have become the primary goals of adolescence, now extended in some cases through several careers, relationships, or sexual orientations. The secular self is inherently transient. Modernity urges that identity be chosen individually and intentionally, on the Kantian mandate, "think for yourself." Relying on guidance from or the authority of others is wimpish. Backing on modernity's distrust of the past and trust in oneself, one creates one's own identity and value system without benefit of the wisdom of elders. Schooling encourages students to think independently rather than trust seasoned experience. Indeed, the modern academy is built on this very foundation. Maturity is gauged by individuality and autonomy. Slogans of the youth culture are "question authority," and "never trust anyone over thirty." Distrust of all but oneself is a modern, not a Christian, virtue. Perhaps we might designate the modern virtue self-trust.

While the goal of freedom is empowerment of the self, a side effect may be moral and intellectual vertigo, because secular emancipation does not attend to the initial and intentional formation of the self, to provide it with moral and intellectual resources to use if one gets caught in circumstances calling for emancipation. Neither does it recognize natural fluctuations of intellectual and moral endowment that recognize the need for help in formation. The modern self, exemplified by the Kantian transcendental ego, is so thoroughly autonomous that it cannot admit that not everyone can lead a self-conscious life, spontaneously responding to duty and righteousness. The truth is that most people really do not think as clearly as Kant did and as he assumed others could, too. The late modern expression of the Kantian norm of self-sufficiency has no need for moral and intellectual formation and growth. Perhaps the late twentieth century exhibits decayed modernity.

Neediness and dependency are signs of weakness to the secular sensibility. Even learning in our society may now be viewed as an infringement on self-direction. Education has become largely skills training to a vocational end rather than a means to develop the student's whole self using the texts and traditions of the past. The norm of self-sufficiency of the modern self renders not only education but also, of course, the Christian faith problematic, as it presupposes that everyone needs God in order to develop properly.

Closely allied with the norm of self-sufficiency is the norm of self-construction. The natural self judges the panoply of intellectual and ethical options that pass by, selecting those that fit its temperament, interest, or curiosity. Values are not to be learned from a tradition, and tested and adapted to a variety of circumstances as Aristotle taught, but one's very own values are to be "clarified," according to the standards of humanistic education of the 1970s. Character education is now coming as a corrective to humanistic education. But the fear of "imposing" values now runs wide and deep in our culture. Individuality, and, with the help of Derrida, *différence*, have become a fetish. No society can long endure when morality gives way to personal preference. Indeed, the norm of self-creation is itself a contradiction, for self-formation requires intellectual effort that the natural self eschews in favor of its natural self-expression. So the natural self and the self-constructed self are at odds with one another from the very outset. Freedom construed on the natural model of "just be yourself" and freedom through self-construction collide.

Descartes, a central contributor to the theme of self-sufficiency, lived in a society in epistemic confusion. He decided to doubt everything he had been taught and think his own way to certitude, thus shaping the modern notion of self-respect through individuality. His scion is Holden Caulfield, with the difference that Descartes prudently decided not to throw off the moral values of the society until he found something with which to replace them, which, by the way, he never did.[4]

4. J. D. Salinger, *The Catcher in the Rye* (Boston: Little, Brown & Co., 1945).

Yet we really speak out of only one side of our mouths when speaking of the self-sufficiency of the self. For as noted above, modern dignity is dependent on the respect accorded one by others. This weakness in the modern ideology is now taking the lives of inner-city children who have mistaken fear for respect and who have a distorted notion of human dignity as power over others. The craving for respect from his buddies that drove Augustine to ravage that famous pear tree belies the modern claim to self-sufficiency, for it reveals an insecurity in the self that must be constantly assuaged by external reinforcement and personal power.[5] Rousseau himself understood this as the primary factor that distorts the natural self. This supports the suggestion that trust in the sovereign self is naive. What will liberate the children suffering from these distortions of human selfhood? Secular modernity assumed that moral, intellectual, and emotional maturity were natural and spontaneous, so that intentional formation was unnecessary at best and oppressive at worst. The crisis of modernity suggests that this assumption was naive.

In addition to insecurities in the self, the recent discussion of the social construction of the self also belies the norm of self-construction. Popular culture is coming to be recognized as an agent of social construction, as concern about television and film violence attest. If popular culture and the standards of the marketplace come to be seen as having negative influences on character development, it becomes evident that the theme of self-formation must be tempered. It is not really a question of whether the self is formed by the society or the inner resources of the self, but how these sources of the self work or fail to work together.

Further evidence of the fragility of the modern self is found in popular talk of self-esteem. Educators speak of children who have

---

5. Augustine, *The Confessions of St. Augustine* (New York: Mentor/New American Library, 1963).

a poor or a healthy self-image. By that they mean on one hand that just being themselves deserves honor and respect, while on the other hand commending a sense of power that arises from accomplishment. Rousseau pointed out that experiences of early childhood establish self-esteem, and so we ever more effusively celebrate children to be sure that they feel good about themselves. We teach wealthy children that the world is their oyster, that they can accomplish whatever they set their minds to, yet we pay scant attention to their moral and spiritual formation, allowing popular culture to have a strong hand in their formation. But the entertainment culture fails to encourage discipline and hard work (except for athletics and music). Nor does it prepare youngsters for disappointment, unfairness, or the sinfulness they will encounter in themselves and others, for the modern worldview lacks not only a doctrine of sin but also a doctrine of grace. Middle-class parents are careful not to quash adolescent girls' intellectual abilities, and so they assiduously cultivate their daughters' gifts in sports, music, art, writing, math, and science, pride in which contributes to their future success. In a competitive, accomplishment-driven society, self-esteem is bolstered by winning, exemplified by competitive sports. It is a contest from which there is no rest.

The conflicting messages of the good, deserving, natural self over against the relentless striving for success are accompanied by the decline of reliance on guilt and shame as instruments of moral formation, for these may damage budding self-esteem. The modern self calls for the pursuit of happiness now articulated as self-actualization or self-realization. Gone is the value of self-control required to avoid wrongdoing. Humanistic psychology, following the hermeneutic of emancipation, suggests that discharge of emotion, now detached from a larger goal of self-mastery, is central to mental health, so that the expression of anger, for example, may be considered therapeutic in itself. The psychological principle beneath all this is that the natural self must be unconstrained in order to flourish. There is no longer a larger context for the self — which God once provided — that values humility and within which a volatile emotion like anger could be modulated or interpreted to a further end.

The romantic-expressive self reaches beyond the popular belief that the expression of emotion is therapeutic to the claim that sexual activity between consenting adults is also appropriate because it is a natural expression of desire. Sexual self-control is no longer considered virtuous. Adolescents are now assumed, sometimes even pressured, to be sexually active at young ages. Sex and alcohol structure social life on many college campuses. The social pressure for sexual conquest and experimentation and alcohol consumption is quite stressful for adolescents, not to mention the dangers it poses. It is but the latest challenge for the autonomous self facing other self-generated selves, vying for respect, power, and affection in a competitive, even brutal, environment. Gone are a healthy respect, even awe, before the power of sex and a genuine respect for one's body. It should not be surprising that sexually transmitted diseases, incest, and date rape are becoming more common.

In addition to the expression of emotion and sexuality to achieve self-realization, the modern self is also expected to be artistically gifted. Stephen Dedalus, James Joyce's autobiographical stand-in, rejected the conventions of morality, school, church, home, and nation to spread his artistic wings, and added a creative component into the assumptions about the modern self.[6] Abraham Maslow introduced this norm of creativity within the purview of normal psychology with his highly influential book, *Toward a Psychology of Being*.[7] Like Descartes, Locke, and Kant, who established the norm

6. James Joyce, *A Portrait of the Artist as a Young Man* (New York: B. W. Huebsch, 1916).
7. Abraham H. Maslow, *Toward a Psychology of Being* (Princeton: Van Nostrand, 1962).

of rationality and clear thinking, Joyce, Maslow, and others projected
a standard of creativity and untrammeled freedom that is vertiginous
for personalities needing structure and guidance.

In a word, by turning from confidence in God to confidence
in itself alone, the secular self proves to be quite alone. It is thrown
on the world to seek its fortune, without history, without guidance,
with scant moral boundaries, and without a framework of meaning
within which to interpret failure and suffering. The modern self is
discouraged from supporting social and political life, for these necessarily place limits on the self and demand compromise, self-
restraint, and even self-sacrifice that are no longer supported by the
culture. Freedom, self-sufficiency, and an expectation of happiness
render it anomic, amoral, asocial, and alone. Having no access to
God, sin, and grace, it has only itself to confide in or worry about.
Families and bonds of community cannot be sustained on this highly
individualistic and morally vacuous basis. This asociality and
amorality are, I suggest, the source of the crisis of modern values.

3

While Moltmann is correct that Christian themes have been used
to promote individualism, Christian theology can offer an alternative to the romantic-expressive self. By dwelling in the dignity of
God, heeding the call and cross of Jesus Christ, and residing in the
body of Christ, Christianity offers a broad theological context and
self-understanding that carry the individual beyond self-fulfillment
and self-gratification. Taken together these three pivots of the Christian self provide a more uplifted goal for life than secularism can
offer.

Christian dignity comes from dwelling in the being of God,
rather than from self-expression or the respect of others. This, not
simply an isolated life of contemplation, is the point of Augustine's

moral psychology in the *De trinitate*.[8] Coming to know God enables us to understand ourselves properly and with greater nobility and happiness than our own abilities can muster, for we are in the divine image. Fitted as we are with all manner of little analogous trinities, we come to understand the purpose of life not in terms of our desires, but in terms of the wisdom of God as we turn to the adoration of God and away from self-gratification. Christian traditions that center the self in God have been interpreted as calling for the denial of self. But what does denial of self mean precisely? It is not that our self is not important, but that in finding our identity in God we turn into a self whose joy is now from and for God. This, rather than a self bent on self-gratification, is a self that is truly and genuinely for itself, its best self.

In his exposition of the doctrine of the Trinity Augustine explained the biblical teaching that we are made in the divine image by means of the trinitarian structure of God, inviting seekers who wish to grow in self-understanding to rethink themselves in this way. By closely associating the teaching on humanity with the teaching on God, Augustine took the position that immediate desire does not have the last word. It is transformed as God leads the seeker to the wisdom that is himself. The primary foundation of the Christian self is its intimacy with God. In light of this perspective, things we previously desired lose their appeal. Turning to God reforms desire and thereby emancipates us from our unloveliness.

In his paper on revaluing modern values Moltmann offered us the standard objection that Augustine's doctrine of God — the so-called psychological model — encourages precisely the individuality and autonomy that contribute to the current modern crisis. But Augustinian individuality is not secular individuality, for it is never detached from transformation as one discovers oneself to be in the

---

8. Augustine, *The Trinity*, The Works of Saint Augustine (Brooklyn: New City Press, 1991).

image of God as others are following suit. On the contrary, the discovery that one's proper self is the image of God constitutes the reconstruction of the self through the practice of self-restraint, retraining of desire, and the cultivation of virtue. The objection that the cultivation of virtue is asocial, however, is I think not an appropriate criticism of Augustine. For the Greco-Roman world, beginning with Plato, believed that a just and wise society requires just and wise citizens. It is the formation of those citizens that modern secularism has neglected. The institutions of the society then are no longer guided by persons who have a theologically developed character and value system, but by persons formed directly by the values of the marketplace itself without an intervening frame of reference.

Paul had worked out a related understanding of Christian self-hood in his teaching that Christ comes to take up residence in the Christian at baptism. Christ's reconciling power becomes the Christian's armor. In fighting the spiritual forces that lead us from righteousness, we grow into new life in Christ, conformed to the image of God in Christ. Belonging to God through dying and rising with Christ in baptism and being sealed by the Holy Spirit set the standard for how one is to conduct oneself, for one's behavior reflects upon God.

The teaching of intimacy with God as the way to a proper self, found in Paul and Augustine and elaborated in the Orthodox tradition, through its doctrine of *theosis,* is not permission to withdraw from the world but is the basis for freedom from the pressures of the world. The modern self, as we have seen, depends — or at least claims to depend — on itself alone. That is the source of its fragility and instability. It is chained to what it can know and do on its own. That instability and fragility are not a problem for the Christian whose surefootedness comes from God. It is probably to the good that different theologians have taught the formation of Christian identity through different doctrines. The variety enables us to grasp the point from different angles. Christian psychology gives us a theological context for the formation of the self. It is a call to lift our eyes from the pavement, to turn our heads from the mirror, for there is another place to dwell. Our identity is not self-constructed but given by God and rooted in the being of God.

Traditionally in the West the cross rather than the Trinity has been the prime locus of Christian devotion. Paul first brought the scandal of the cross into focus. It is perhaps the most delicate theme in Christian thought. Here I concur with critics who point out that it is a teaching that has been complicit in the destruction of God's creatures. The problem is evident as early as 1 Peter 2:18ff., where the author urges slaves to follow Christ's example and endure unjust suffering to gain God's approval. Still, Christians cling to the cross of Christ because, as Paul taught, we are reconciled to God by his death (Rom. 4–5) and called to extend that ministry of reconciliation that makes all things new (2 Cor. 5:16ff.). Christians cannot leave the modern world to itself, not because it would take Christians down with it, but because the cross will not permit it. Paul's teaching of the cross, unlike later dogmatic exegeses, is not a technical explanation of how God works out forgiveness of sin. It is rather a fact, a deed, an event, in light of which we must rethink ourselves, allowing our natural self to be reshaped by a radical understanding of strength and power authorized by God's condescending compassion.

Perhaps the point at which Paul speaks most directly of compassion as power is in 1 Corinthians 1:18-31. It is a passage that stands in tension with the 1 Peter material mentioned above. The wisdom of the cross discloses power as the reconciling work that turns enemies into sisters and brothers and forgives sin. Those in Christ know that the cross frees people from the categories of status and power that the world uses to enslave us. It means that we are free from the struggle to be first, to be best, to be in control of others and instead to be in control of ourselves and the power to rescue others. The cross points out that what looks like strength in

the world's terms is weakness, and what looks like humiliation —
God's humility in becoming us and dying on a cross — displays real
dignity and nobility: the power of compassion. True strength is the
power not to control others but to give them new life. In submitting
to the wisdom of the cross we achieve true freedom.

Paul's message of the cross is not simply freedom from the
powers of the world, but it is directed freedom. The message of the
cross is not cause for a private celebration of justification or forgiveness of individual sins. Nor is it only freedom from legal constraint.
Nor is it only existential freedom from the sirens of the world. The
message of the cross also directs Christians to their new life as slaves
to righteousness, slaves to God, as Paul spells this out in Romans.
Perhaps this is where the disagreement comes between the Christian and the modern self. The Christian is bound to God and
righteousness while the modern self's resource is itself. The Christian
self is guided and directed while the secular self is on its own.

The third of the three distinguishing pivots of the Christian self
is its belonging in the body of Christ. Divine guidance takes place
in the community of the faithful. While the secular emancipation
narrative encourages the self to free itself from formative and social-
izing influences that might thwart self-expression, the Christian
seeks formation in the midst of an ordered community in order to
prepare itself for a cross-defined life that may move across the grain
of the dominant culture. This is symbolized by the ancient baptismal
custom of receiving the newly baptized immediately into the body
of the congregation, where they are officially welcomed and receive
the body and blood of Christ for the first time, having been excluded
from these rites as catechumens. Sacramental confession, spiritual
direction, and the Lord's Supper support and encourage the life of
faith and righteousness, as does public worship. Study of scripture,
the lives of the saints, writings of honored spiritual guides, and
perhaps even of a theologian now and again surround Christians
with a transtemporal community in order to fortify them for Chris-

tian living in a world that no longer understands Christian claims and virtues.

These three points of the Christian self — the Trinity, the call and cross of Christ, and residence in the body of Christ — emancipate the self from the limits of its own striving and form a Christian identity. It is primarily the recognition of the need for divine guidance that marks it off from the romantic-expressive self that no longer understands the Christian claim that we need God.

If finding one's identity in God provides an independent basis from which to address the decay of modernity, Christians must first think through how that might best be undertaken in our present circumstance. The claim that we (really) need God must again be rendered intelligible to an age that may no longer understand those words. The need for formation and transformation of the self must be articulated as the emancipation that it properly is. The values of humility and self-control must again be spoken of in a way that calms the fear of authoritarianism spurred by the excesses of late medieval devotionalism that still haunt the modern psyche. In short, what is called for is the reclamation of an autonomous Christian voice that can interpret Christian commitments to a culture still in reaction against repressive authoritarianism that no longer understands any set of commitments larger than the autonomous self. Christian theology must explain how submission to God, though difficult, is not necessarily oppressive or repressive but can be genuinely helpful and liberating.

Modern secularism is in certain ways a reaction against the Christian self as understood in the Middle Ages. Then the assumption was that self-hatred was the only appropriate stance before the wrath of God. In order to extirpate the ghost of that era from later sensibilities moderns, especially late moderns, have gone to extremes in throwing off all external authority and standards of judgment. Whereas the medievals and earlier monastics sought to destroy self and the natural needs of the body, moderns have glorified each point in turn. Where they espoused poverty, we accumulate wealth. Where they honored chastity, late moderns celebrate sex. Where they cultivated humility and obedience, we cultivate individuality and self-fulfillment.

The hyperindividualism, crisis of the family, vertigo of youth, and weakening of the bonds of public life may be understood in part as caused by a violent reaction against the excesses of a particular interpretation of the Christian self that so focused on the wrath of God that life was dominated by guilt and anxiety and the self paralyzed with fear. The consequent rejection of authority, transcendent values, and even the virtues of humility and self-restraint that characterize our own search for emancipation may now in turn have reached an extreme and themselves be coming under scrutiny. Perhaps it is time to see that the reaction against the authoritarian excesses of the Western church, while understandable, has nevertheless spun off ills of its own.

4

I have argued along with Moltmann that the crisis of modernity is a crisis of the modern self. But I have argued contra Moltmann that Christians cannot address the crisis unless they have an independent place to stand. To this end I have argued for the reformulation of the Christian self, pointing out flaws in the secular self that I believe now contribute to the moral and social breakdown of society. The secular self is inherently lonely and given to suspicion, having only itself to rely upon. The individuality of the modern self provides few bridges to community, whether for comfort and companionship or as a moral plumbline against which one could be called to account before others. By contrast, the Christian self, which I have only briefly sketched here, finds its dignity in God and its community in the body of Christ. It is more stable than the modern self and